PRAISE FOR *CRISIS* ⸺⸺⸺⸺⸺

Through deft storytelling, *Crisis Communications and the Art of Making Nothing Happen* by Joe Diorio is an engaging book highlighting how planning for the worst helps companies, organizations, and government agencies communicate with the public during a crisis. Unlike dry textbooks on the subject, Joe Diorio draws the reader infrom the start where he details surviving a gunman's deadly workplace attack and continues with the use of a fictionalized case, based on real-life scenarios. It is a must-read for those in the crisis communication field.

—Maureen Boyle, Journalism Program Director at Stonehill College

I learned about crisis communications the hard way, through crises, before I met and was lucky enough to work with Joseph Diorio. Of the many things I learned from him, I was always most impressed with his ability to turn a narrative from reactive to proactive and defensive to positive. It's probably equal parts skill and mojo, but if anyone can help you be better it's Joe.

—David Gittelman, Vice President of
Marketing & Communications at Reliance Matrix

No one wants tragedy to strike, but you'll be glad you read this book and began your due diligence establishing an action plan in the event it does.

In this must-read for aspiring and veteran communications professionals alike, Joe Diorio takes a critical subject like a mass shooting at a vulnerable workplace and, through pulse-racing and witty narration, provides a digestible and comprehensive crisis communications template for those not just on the frontlines but also for those sitting in the change-maker seats in the boardroom, some of whom might be thinking, "Nah, we don't need this" or "we'll have to get to it later."

To them, I issue this saying by Benjamin Franklin that remains as resonant in 2024 as it was in Franklin's time: "By failing to prepare, you are preparing to fail." And I recommend Diorio's book as their golden guide map to preventative action measures a business can take right away in a modern world.

Joe Diorio is the Brene Brown of PR and communications. I'm recommending this book to everyone I know who cares about the future of their company and humanity in general.

—ifnotnowwhen83, Barnes and Noble reviewer

No one wants to deal with a crisis, but bad things can happen at any time. In a modern world with information, rumors, and opinions at our fingertips Joe proves that companies need to be prepared to take charge of any situation. He provides real resources for communications teams to utilize - some programs I've never heard of before! As a former TV reporter, I know a lot about the "other side" Joe's book makes me excited to learn more about crisis planning and work collaboratively with my team and clients on being prepared for any situation. Even the seasoned communications professional may benefit from this read - I';m looking forward to sharing with my colleagues!

—Rachel AS, Barnes and Noble reviewer

As communications professionals, we are trained to be several steps ahead. To expect - and be prepared to respond to - the unexpected. But sometimes it's hard to understand how our plans will play out in real life.

Joe provides a terrifying yet unfortunately very real scenario and illustrates how a crisis could be handled from a communications standpoint with proper preparation and crisis communication planning.

If your organization doesn't have an (updated!) crisis communications plan in place, this book is a great reminder and guide to help get you started.

—Kb715, Barnes and Noble Reviewer

CRISIS COMMUNICATIONS

AND THE ART OF MAKING NOTHING HAPPEN

ISBN: 978-0-8253-1036-2 (paperback)
ISBN: 978-0-8253-0914-4 (eBook)

For inquiries about volume orders, please contact:
Beaufort Books
sales@beaufortbooks.com

Published in the United States by Beaufort Books
www.beaufortbooks.com

Distributed by Midpoint Trade Books a division of Independent Publisher Group
https://www.ipgbook.com/

Interior design by Frances K. Fragela Rivera
Cover Design by Frances K. Fragela Rivera

Printed in the United States of America

Note: This manuscript is the intellectual property of Joseph J. Diorio

CRISIS COMMUNICATIONS

AND THE ART OF MAKING NOTHING HAPPEN

BY JOE DIORIO

CONTENTS

FOREWORD
By Jeff Butera

The best press secretary of my lifetime had the benefit of Aaron Sorkin writing her words.

Her name was C.J. Cregg, expertly played by Allison Janney for seven captivating seasons on Sorkin's hit drama "The West Wing."

C.J. was intelligent and poised, a master of the English language and a formidable verbal jouster. But what made C.J. a truly effective press secretary was her embrace of a simple reality:

There is often a responsibility to your community to be honest, transparent and forthright.

You may not want to answer questions, but sometimes you should. You may not care to share information, but sometimes you ought to. You may not believe transparency would be best for your company, but sometimes secrecy would be worse.

C.J. understood this. In fact, her mindset is precisely encapsulated in six words she utters during a Season 3 episode:

"Information breeds trust. Silence breeds fear."

I think those six words could be an effective subtitle for Joe Diorio's *Crisis Communications and the Art of Making Nothing Happen* Joe's book—while also a gripping read—provides a blueprint for crisis communications that would have C.J. Cregg nodding her head with approval.

I must confess: I've never seen crisis communications from Joe's side. Instead, I've spent 20+ years as a reporter and anchor at television news stations around the country, seeking information and sound bites from people like Joe, rather than deciding which information and sound bites to release.

But I've covered enough tragedies from 'my side' to know what's most effective on 'the other side:'

1. You can't say nothing. The information vacuum will get filled. Wouldn't you rather be the entity that fills it, rather than staying silent and allowing someone else to tell 'your story?'

2. Saying nothing makes it look like you're doing nothing. The public does not expect you to be able to answer every question, have every problem solved, consider every contingency and right every wrong. But it matters to them that you're doing … something. Take action and then share those actions with the public.

3. The best communicators have a plan. They have already considered how to approach crisis situations, decided which information they can safely release and determined how best to get their message out.

I'm encouraged to see Joe preaching the same things in this book. In short: He gets it.

We may be coming at these nightmare scenarios from 'different sides,' but I'm certain we'd agree with C.J. Cregg on those powerful six words about how "information breeds trust" but "silence breeds fear."

The words that follow in Joe's book serve as an excellent master plan for achieving that.

Jeff Butera has worked as a journalist for more than 20 years, reporting and anchoring the news at stations in Tampa, Phoenix, Jacksonville, Fort Myers, Huntsville and Gainesville. He's also the author of "Write Like You Talk: A Guide To Broadcast News Writing."

FOREWORD
By Jen Crompton

A riddle: What are two words that are equivalent to saying you are guilty as charged?

The answer: No comment.

As innocent as those words appear to be, they are the antithesis of what any good public relations strategist would advise in any situation – namely, in a crisis. That's because perception is reality these days, and a "no comment" response elicits guilt, even if that is not the case.

However, companies still use those two words as a default response when they are unprepared and a crisis upends the business, bringing with it a cloud of uncertainty and immediate chaos. The crisis triggers a communication frenzy, and clear, consistent messaging is too often, well, neither clear nor consistent. For some, activating the "no comment" response could end up being the nail in the proverbial coffin (or the hole that sinks the ship, which may or may not be worth saving).

This is precisely why Joe Diorio offers a detailed—and gripping—perspective of a crisis situation and how it was handled and, in another case, badly mishandled. He gives readers an in-depth look into the importance of crisis PR and real-world strategies to plan and execute during what can be some of the most volatile and perilous situations a company may face.

With Joe's background in P.R., he sheds light on how multiple missteps can turn into a giant mess. And even though companies struggle to prioritize crisis communication plans (because who really wants to believe a crisis will happen on their watch), flying by the seat of your pants in the face of a moment of trust is, by far, the worst-case scenario.

Written as a narrative, this book is perfect for any communications professional who wants to understand how to truly be prepared for and navigate a crisis with poise and honesty (and without losing their job or going down with the ship). It offers insight into working with stakeholders and, ultimately, which mistakes to avoid along the way.

As Joe says, "If the press cannot get a story from the source, then they will instead make their own story from available sources." Any P.R. practitioner will back this up and add that "controlling the narrative" is the best way to get out with the least amount of damage.

Jen Crompton has worked in strategic communications and P.R. for over 20 years, helping small and mid-sized businesses define their brand, refine their messaging, and navigate the wild world of media relations. Jen is an entrepreneur and motivational speaker, and co–author of the children's book, "Fuel Your Best," which is about her other passions – fitness and inclusivity.

For every public relations pro who created a crisis communications plan, thanks.

And for those P.R. pros who couldn't create a plan because their clients never seemed to get around to it, this is for you, too.

MANAGING THE LIFE CYCLE OF A CRISIS

1. Modify and Notify

2. Activate the Communication Response Team

3. Gather the Facts

4. Formulate the Response

5. Identify Stakeholders

6. Deliver the Message

7. Monitor and Correct

8. Update and Follow Up

9. Debrief and Evaluate

10. Recover

A MEA CULPA
From the author

I was shot at by a crazed gunman during a mass shooting. He missed. I'm naturally as ugly as I appear. (Yes, I joke about it. The memory can be horrific if I dwell on it too much.) But he did not miss three of my coworkers.

This happened on May 28, 1982.

Over forty years later, I still have two distinct memories of that day. The first was the understandable fear of possibly dying by gunshot. I was convinced I had arrived at the moment where I would die as I lay on the floor under the conference table in the room where my coworkers and I hid, repeating the Lord's Prayer over and over. For me, the end wasn't near. It was here.

The second, less obvious emotion was frustration and anger with my employer, the IBM Corporation. I wasn't angry because the shooting happened. I was angry because I was severely criticized a few days later for doing what I thought was my job.

About the shooting:

Several hundred of my coworkers and I were victims of the rampage of an out-of-control man, a former employee of IBM, holding and firing two guns. He drove his Lincoln Town Car through the glass doors of an IBM office building in Bethesda, Maryland where I worked at the time. He emerged from the car and shot at anything and everything, killing three persons and wounding seven.

He fired in my direction as I stood outside of a coworker's office. Just before that moment I heard Audrey, my admin, screaming, "There's a guy with a gun, and he's shooting the place up!" I saw Audrey running toward me and about 20 feet behind her was a man in a ski mask wearing what appeared to be a U.S. Army surplus jacket. His choice of a coat was strange; it was the Friday before Memorial Day, and the weather was hot and humid outside. (Yes, I was dwelling on trivial facts at that moment.)

He fired the gun—I think it was a shotgun—and the bullets hit the wall where I would have been standing had I not ducked. I saw the damage to the wall the next day when I returned to the building to retrieve my suit jacket, car keys, and wallet. I had left my jacket, which contained my keys and wallet, hanging on the back of my office door. There was certainly no time to retrieve them that day.

Audrey, myself, and three other coworkers all hid in a conference room. Someone in our little group knew that room had a door with a padlock to it; the other doors in the building were intentionally left without locks. In 1982, IBM had an "open door" policy, meaning your door should be open and always unlocked. And since virtually no office doors had locks, that was an easy rule to follow.

More than three hours passed before a police S.W.A.T. team freed us from the building. The police were going door-to-door, slowly opening each to see if the other side of the door had IB-Mers hiding in there or if the room was the den of a violent man with multiple weapons. When I heard a knock at the door of our hiding place and the voice of the police, I immediately opened it. My coworkers later admitted they were too afraid to open the door. When I finally opened the door, the first thing I saw was a shotgun. The weapon was wielded by a police officer who calmly and forcefully told me to show my hands, come out of the room, and exit the building while keeping my hands above my head.

I wasn't shot that day, so I wasn't considered a victim. And I don't consider myself a victim, either. But I nevertheless became a part of a mass shooting. It's a club no one wants to join, but it is a club that sadly has a growing membership. The *Gun Violence Archive* estimates that, as of July 4, 2024, there were 261 mass shootings in the United States. It is an out-of-control problem.

By the way, since only two people died on the actual day of the shooting (a third died from injuries later), this incident does not meet the U.S. Congressional Research Service's 2015 criteria of a mass shooting. This report says four or more persons must die before an incident is considered a mass shooting. Dr. Garen Wintemute of the University of California at Davis, who himself is a gun violence researcher (imagine having that on one's resume) contends there is no right or wrong when it comes to defining a mass shooting. Good thing, too. Try explaining to the family of someone who died that their loved one technically was not in a mass shooting. But I'm getting off topic here.

The events of this day predate the term "going postal." Google Ngram notes those two words are an American English slang term used for descriptive purposes when someone becomes uncontrollably angry, and that term would not become common in our lexicon until about 1991. Yet this shooter definitely went postal.

Also, this unforgettable day happened before the phrase "mass shooting" became a common idiom. (Again, according to Google Ngram, that term did not become common until 2005.) The incident is therefore a precursor to the bloody mayhem we seem to have become accustomed to. It also happened before shooters, as scholars like Jaclyn Schildkraut, Ph.D. (SUNY Oswego) point out, became media celebrities. This and the fact it was so long ago is probably why so few people remember the name of the shooter. (Edward Thomas Mann, in case you were wondering.)

As I mentioned, my second memory of that day was feeling victimized by and a little angry with my employer. I was not feeling angry because I had been shot at. I was angry because I was raked over the coals by IBM's top executives for doing my job. It took me forty years to realize this, but my coworkers in Bethesda were most likely the recipients of IBM's corporate ire because there was little or no crisis communications planning in advance of this incident. At least no plan anyone in Bethesda knew about. And that was not necessarily anyone's fault.

IBM in 1982 excelled at product publicity. My coworkers and I comprised a regional product publicity office there in Bethesda; a "Regional Press Office" was the term IBM used to describe who we were and what we did. We were solely focused on product publicity—that is, find ways to promote how IBM products were used. For example, just a few weeks before this shooting, I had placed a story in the fledgling newspaper *USA Today* about a gym in downtown Washington, D.C. that was using an IBM Personal Computer to run body fat analyses on clients. That application is commonplace today, but it was a cutting-edge use of technology back in 1982.

But managing communications after a crisis was a horse of a different color for Big Blue, a onetime nickname for IBM, referring to the blue color on one panel of its mainframe computers. When Tuesday morning came about – remember, the shooting happened on the Friday leading into Memorial Day weekend – my coworkers and I returned to our offices and the building looked like nothing had happened. A whirlwind of activity had taken place over that weekend as damages to the building – walls, windows, carpeting, and doorways – all were repaired, probably at a price that would make anyone's head spin. But things did not look or seem the same for us in the Regional Press Office.

There were scores of press inquiries (PIs) waiting for us and more on the way.

Fielding an array of questions from the press was a routine part of our jobs; we had boilerplate answers for questions like: "How many people work for IBM in Washington?" ("We don't comment on employee statistics," is the serious answer. "About half," is the answer we shared amongst ourselves.), "What government agency is your biggest customer?" (Probably the Department of Defense, but we don't give out contact numbers.), and "Do you have any comment on IBM doing business in South Africa?" ("You'll need to talk to our corporate offices about that.") All normal stuff. But I doubt anyone could have anticipated the volume of calls and requests we started getting the Monday after the shooting.

There were requests to enter the building and video record news stories. Requests to interview random employees to see how they felt about returning to work at the site of a bloody experience. Requests to do live "remotes" from inside the building. Reporters who were not on the phone were on the sidewalk outside of the building, waiting for a chance to come inside. This was a level of interest no one with IBM could have anticipated. There were four of us in this regional IBM press office, and we were quickly feeling overwhelmed by the volume of calls we were getting.

IBM's corporate offices in Armonk, New York had provided a simple one-sentence statement for use with all PIs related to the shooting: "We continue to feel deep sorrow for the victims of the shooting and their families. We will have no further comment." That bit of stonewalling was not holding up very well against the nonstop surge of PIs.

If the press cannot get a story from the source, then they will instead make their own story from available resources. Reporters on the sidewalk flagged down employees as they arrived at work, asking questions. Others sought out the families of the victims for comment. There was this thirst for a story, and if

IBM was not going to quench it the press would look for an oasis elsewhere.

Sometime around mid-afternoon on June 1, the executives in IBM's corporate offices found out how many inquiries we were getting. They decided we weren't doing our jobs and chewed us out big time. Even though it was the corporate office personnel who wrote the standby statement we were using.

My anger at the time was real, but I held no grudge against IBM. The anger was more from a feeling of, "Hey, I just got shot at, and you're yelling at me?"

Rather than just saying, "We'll take it from here," we received several messages from headquarters that were tantamount to, "What the hell are YOU doing?" We felt we were doing our jobs, that's what. Corporate headquarters felt otherwise. I didn't appreciate the anger coming my way from headquarters. My co-workers and I were being careful as we answered press questions, and none of our responses put IBM in a bad light.

After receiving a verbal reaming, IBM assigned day-to-day press responsibilities to another P.R. office it maintained in Washington, D.C. It was an operation that was a part of a division that did work with the U.S. Department of Defense. For nearly a year they served as IBM's spokespersons for this story, basically saying little more than what was in the original stand-by statement.

My emotional wounds from IBM's corporate office's verbal reaming healed quickly enough. Today I laugh at the memory (of being yelled at, not shot at) more than anything else.

IBM did not have a crisis communications plan for the events of May 28, 1982. (Or if one existed, it was not shared with the regional press office in Bethesda.) There was no single spokesperson identified until after it became apparent that one was needed. There was no obvious plan to communicate with constituents (especially customers) about what happened in

Bethesda and whether plans and procedures were in place to prevent it from happening elsewhere (and in 1982 IBM had offices throughout the country). There was no mention of the shooting in the company annual report for 1982. The CEO of IBM, John Opel, visited the site over the weekend as repairs were taking place, and preparations were taken to accommodate his visit. There was no press involved with his visit. In a sense, the event was pushed under the proverbial rug.

Looking back at that time and comparing it to what happened with mass shootings in more recent times, I am struck by the positive impact good communication planning can have for a company.

For example, 40 years ago, IBM streamlined the process of paying medical bills, significantly reducing the paperwork someone would have to complete. IBM also hired psychiatrists to be on-site in the building to talk to anyone who was experiencing any degree of post-traumatic stress. Next, IBM negotiated an agreement with the Montgomery County, Maryland district attorney's office to conduct weekly updates regarding the status of the trial against Mann (who eventually pleaded guilty and later on hung himself while in prison).

IBM spent a fortune fixing the building quickly so that it bore no sign of damage when everyone returned to work four days after things hit the fan. By Tuesday morning, June 1, as people returned to work there was no sign that a shooting and a loss of life had happened. Damaged plaster walls were repaired or replaced, and a fresh coat of paint was applied to the entire building, not just the areas damaged by gunshots. Broken glass was replaced. The lobby was completely repaired, including replacing carpeting where the Lincoln Town Car had sat after crashing through the glass doors. Workers on this fast-track repair event could have most likely charged a fortune in overtime. IBM paid every bill. No questions asked.

The only faint sign of trauma in the building when everyone returned to work on Tuesday were the glass double doors that were destroyed when Mann drove his car through them. They were custom-made ten-foot-high glass doors. There was a double set of these doors at the north and south entrances to the building (Mann drove through the south entrance); the space in-between the doors acted as a kind of vestibule to keep wind, leaves, and other things from blowing into the lobby. Since the replacement doors were a special order ("You could just about name your price for those," one person close to the reconstruction of the building told me. In reality, someone probably did.), the new doors were not ready for Tuesday's return to work. Instead, one set of the ten-foot-high glass doors from the north side of the building were used to temporarily replace the shattered entrance at the south side. But one had to consciously think about the absence of the second doorway before realizing what had been done.

Those four things—paying medical bills, having assistance on site, providing frequent detailed updates on the trial, and making sure everything appeared back to normal—would be considered feathers in any company's hat today. Yet IBM did not speak a word of it to anyone on the outside.

IBM was never defined by what happened on May 28, 1982, but it was a changed company in subtle ways. Concrete bollards soon stood at the base of the sidewalk outside of the building. Designed for good looks, the bollards were there to prevent another car from jumping onto the sidewalk and entering the lobby. Eventually bollards became "de rigueur" design elements on most buildings in the country. The company was always good at managing human resources issues, but extra care was needed after the shooting. Psychologists were on site at the building should anyone need to express themselves to a professional, and new, more flexible (albeit temporary) work schedules were allowed for people who felt they needed time away from the site of the tragedy.

In the four decades since May 28, 1982 we have seen how mass shooting events are communicated by the businesses, the people involved, and interested parties. There were live tweets from the Las Vegas mass shooting in 2019, and a shooter at a bank in Louisville, Kentucky live streamed the event themselves. Police departments prepare standby tweets for use in a variety of crisis and near-crisis situations. Schools have partial and total lockdown procedures and active shooter drills. Members of Congress and the National Rifle Association have their "thoughts and prayers" statements.

It's easy to see crisis plans in action today.

Fast forward nearly 40 years to September 23, 2021, and a mass shooting at a Kroger grocery store in Collierville, Tennessee[13]. There, a disgruntled employee entered that store, armed with a handgun, killing one person. When the store reopened several weeks later, after the damage to the store was repaired and law enforcement officials had completed their investigations, there were marching bands, speeches from politicians, and a more positive vibe that was communicated through events, and live TV. The message being sent that day was: "We're back, we're stronger than ever, and this incident does not define us."

Three years before the Kroger incident, a Waffle House in Nashville was the site of a mass shooting where four persons were killed by a man wielding a semiautomatic weapon. The restaurant was temporarily closed for police investigations and repairs. When it reopened less than a week later there was a celebratory atmosphere inside. Too, the company owning Waffle House pledged to give a month's worth of sales to the victims' families.

Again, with Waffle House the message clearly being conveyed was: "We're strong and resilient, and we are not going anywhere."

The planning and implementation Kroger and Waffle House put into their re-opening strategies grew out of conscious efforts to put a face on a tragedy. In each case there was a plan to identify the situation, activate a team, maintain clear and accurate communications with stakeholders, and to have a plan to recover, which are all hallmarks of solid crisis communications planning.

I wrote this book to provide a good read for the casual reader looking for something with an edginess and action to it. I also wrote it with communications professionals in mind; those who must work to create, maintain, and update communications plans ... things that are still often considered a burden to create, pointless to maintain, and something that ultimately belongs in the "we'll never use this" category.

Let's take a look at how this all can play out.

INTRODUCTION
Based on a True Story

With two guns positioned on the car seat next to him, Mel Tomlinson was going to take revenge on Trask International, his former employer.

And Trask's public relations department was ready for him. They had a crisis communications plan.

Don't get the wrong idea. Trask's P.R. department didn't have an invisible shield a la *Star Trek* that would deploy before Tomlinson showed up with guns a-blazing and deflect each and every shot he took. And no one on the communications staff had a secret identity as a spandex-clad superhero, able to swat away bullets as Tomlinson fired his weapons.

No, people were still going to die, and the office building Tomlinson was about to attack would be damaged so badly that a small army of contractors would be needed to make repairs over the course of a three-day weekend. No, the planning and preparation that went into creating Trask's crisis communications plans wouldn't stop Tomlinson from shooting and killing several people and killing another by running them over with his SUV. There would be nearly $1 million in property damage because of Tomlinson's actions, even more in medical expenses for the injured. Normal business operations would be interrupted for several days.

Despite the existence of a crisis communications plan, all of the carnage, all of the damage was still going to happen.

But because Trask's public relations team implemented crisis communications planning, a lot of good things were also going to happen.

Trask employees, customers, stakeholders, and anyone doing business with Trask were informed about what was going on. No one had to guess. Instead of people making up their own stories, there was abundant compassion toward the company because of what happened.

No one on social media or in the press framed the incident as Trask's fault.

The media coverage of the incident did not focus on a Trask spokesperson. There was no "Trask Face" in the news. That meant public opinion was not swayed by an opinion of whomever was doing the talking. Trask was viewed as a business, trying to get back to business after a horrific event took place.

Work as usual—or as usual as can be—resumed faster than anyone anticipated.

Sure, social media posts would generate a geyser of good and bad opinions about what happened. But the clamor over the mass shooting would die down within a day or two. The anger machine that feeds social media soon needed something else to feed its unlimited appetite.

In fact, because crisis plans were in place, Trask, the local police department, the local school board (there is a high school right next to the building where Tomlinson did his deed) and even the gun lobby emerged unscathed by the rumor maw that can consume the court of public opinion.

And, by the way, businesses that did not plan for a crisis suffered their own consequences even though Tomlinson didn't fire a single shot at them.

The planning helped frame the story for Trask; a frame that said, "Yes, we know this happened. It's awful. And we will do everything we can to make things right and take care of the people involved, the people who do business with us, and the people who are interested in what we do. We are not defined by what happened."

Crises happen. But how they are handled makes all the difference in the world.

For Trask, the benefits of planning unfolded with one angry employee who finally snapped.

Part of the title of this book is "The Art of Making Nothing Happen." That's often how communications professionals describe good public affairs and crisis communications planning. Planning for a crisis involves having in-depth conversations about a lot of "what if" scenarios, and it is easy to become mentally sidetracked when the mindset of "aw, none of this is really going to happen to us" kicks in.

But bad stuff can kick a company in the proverbial behind. In 1990, a British Petroleum (BP) subsidiary was at the center of a substantial oil spill off of Huntington Beach, California, spewing about 130,000 gallons of oil into the ocean. Despite the substantial mess, BP was not chastised in the court of public opinion because the company put repair operations into overdrive, cleaning up the spill and getting the beach back to normal. Daytime talk show host Phil Donahue filmed a segment of his TV show from Huntington Beach, lauding BP for its cleanup efforts. BP's CEO even went on the Today Show to flat-out say the spill was BP's fault.

Nowadays almost no one remembers that oil spill. But mention "Deepwater Horizon" and BP's name will be dragged through dirtier mud than the oil that was spilled from that incident.

The difference was a good crisis response. During the Huntington Beach incident BP's chief executive officer did multiple public appearances, accepting responsibility for the spill. In contrast, people remember Tony Hayward, CEO of British Petroleum during the Deepwater Horizon crisis, saying he just wanted his life back. Not surprisingly, he was raked over the coals for that comment in the court of public opinion.

Crisis plans make a difference. Getting one finished is sometimes a ride of its own.

THE CRISIS

INSIDE MEL TOMLINSON'S SUV
May 24, 2019 | 10:30 a.m.

Mel Tomlinson was angry. He had spent seventeen years of his life with Trask International, Inc., a nationwide IT/cloud consulting company (yes, calling it "International" when its work is only domestic is a contradiction in terms), and now he felt like that time was wasted.

He planned on being there longer than seventeen years, but he was fired for missing his sales quota. He spent one year looking for work. Well, looking for work when he wasn't at home drinking or arguing with his wife, that is.

Tomlinson's lengthy unemployment—Trask fired him in 2017—and substance abuse brought out his worst characteristics. He was battling personal demons, and the demons were winning. Alcohol and a short fuse on his temper did nothing to overcome a longstanding laissez-faire work attitude.

Tomlinson disdainfully thought about the milquetoast guy from human resources who sat in the conference room with Mel, telling him he was being fired—well, HR people hate using the word fired. This guy used words like "relieved," "change in course," "new direction," and on and on. Mel later looked it up and learned there are nearly 260 synonyms and antonyms for the word "fired" in the dictionary.

No, the HR talking head didn't say fired. He did say Mel's issues—God forbid he should use the words "internal demons"—were the reason he was being let go. They needed to be managed, he said. "It's an opportunity for a fresh start," said the smiling jerk.

That's "Trask speak," Tomlinson told himself. "Care for the individual" was a longstanding company sloganeering piece of shit line everyone at Trask International used. And the HR rep had the nerve to lay that on him as he delivered the "we're sorry, Mel, but this isn't working out" news.

"It's for the best for everyone," the HR lackey said. The words hung over him like the late spring humidity. How was this for the best for him? For his wife?

From his perspective, all the problems the HR lackey went on about, all the "issues" Tomlinson was told he had were Trask's fault. Whatever accomplishments he had had on the job went unnoticed or unrewarded.

And Trask was the reason why. *That* led to the booze, the drugs, and only served to exasperate his short temper.

Trask was the reason he lost his job.

Trask's unreasonable sales quotas were a nightmare to meet.

Trask's lousy sales training—where he was frightened into an inability to make decisions—was the root of the problem, not him.

Care for the individual. A positive outlook. Tomlinson kept repeating the lines. Both are longstanding jargon Trask used. It dates back to the very early days of the company when it was more of a mom-and-pop operation than McDonald's. Still, as is often said, the phrase has staying power; it resonates regardless of when it is used.

Don't fuck with Mickey D's, he thought. *I may still need a job.*

He stopped at that thought, glanced at the two guns in the front seat, then returned his gaze to the road. Sometimes that corporate jargoning doesn't translate to everyday use. Not in Tomlinson's case. *Well, someone will need a job.*

Trask International was the reason he drank. Anyone putting up with the crap he faced had to blow off steam somehow, and after work happy hours with coworkers was a survival tactic, not just leisure activity. Although recently there were more random barflies and fewer Traskers joining Mel for happy hours.

Trask International was the reason his personal finances were a train wreck. He used to lease a new BMW every other year, writing it off as a business expense. Now he's driving a used Lincoln SUV. Although he figured out that the SUV would be useful. It can do zero to 60 in less than five seconds so said the sales rep at Aracae Motors where Mel bought the SUV. The salesman—"John" was his name—said the vehicle's towing power was pretty good, too.

Those two facts were all he needed to know about the car. His wife badgered him about buying the car. His wife. His marriage. It was a wreck. And Trask, too, was the reason his marriage was in shambles.

Trask. Nothing good was coming from that outfit.

Trask was going to pay. A pistol grip shotgun and a Glock semi-automatic in the front seat of the useful SUV were the receipts for that payment.

So, at 10:30 a.m. that day he got in the SUV and drove from his home in Darnestown, in northern Montgomery County, Maryland, to Trask International's Bethesda offices. He didn't work there; he was a remote worker since he was in sales. Still, the Bethesda office was a good, high-profile location. Everyone talked about the "rusty bucket," a friendly reference to the building on Udell Road with the exterior finish that constantly looked rusty. Someone once addressed a piece of mail from California, writing only "Trask, Rust Bucket, Bethesda, Maryland" and the letter arrived. That familiarity made the Bethesda office a good, high-profile location.

At 11:28 a.m., after negotiating traffic around a flipped car on the Capital Beltway, Tomlinson turned left off of Udell Road and into the driveway of Trask's suburban Washington, D.C. office building. The three-level building comprised two stories above ground, one below. It housed accounts receivables, human resources, and a few other operations. Below ground, or in the lower level, was the heart of Trask's operation. Accounts receivable/payable. Every invoice was maintained there. Shut that down, and Trask wouldn't know where its next meal was coming from. Or he figured. Trask talked about having its operations in the cloud. No matter, the conduit to the cloud was in that building.

Yeah. Like me, Tomlinson thought. *I don't know where my next meal is coming from, either.*

The building also housed a regional public relations, or P.R., office for Trask. Its function left many employees, including Tomlinson, wondering what the people who worked there really did. Mel had no idea what the "P.R. people" who worked there did. One cynical sales manager called the public relations department "overhead."

Overhead, huh? Tomlinson thought. *I lost my job and the overhead gets to stick around.*

As he made the left turn, he accelerated and swerved right, then left, jumping the sidewalk leading up to the building. Two 15-foot-tall glass doors, part of a 30-foot-high glass-enclosed foyer, were all that stood between the people in the building and the accelerating 4,200-pound weapon he was driving. The low decibel strain on the SUV's 303-horsepower engine assured Tomlinson that he had built up more than enough acceleration.

Inside the atrium sat Carl Wilson at the reception desk/security guard station. Wilson was in his eighth year as the security guard for Bethel Holdings, the company that owned the leased Trask building on Udell Road. He'd taken the job after retiring as a lathe operator at a machine shop in Baltimore. This security guard gig was a way to bring in a little money, or "extra scratch" as he liked to call his paycheck, keep himself busy, and not feel bored. On clear spring days like today he'd enjoy the sunshine coming in through the windows. He was at his post as Tomlinson's SUV was barreling up the sidewalk leading from the parking lot to the doorway. On this day, Wilson wasn't looking up; he instead was focused on a memo reminding security guards to check everyone's employee ID badge when they enter the building. He only looked up when a loud gasp from the woman standing nearby caught his attention. The SUV was already blasting its way through the glass doors when he saw it. It would be the last thing Carl ever saw.

INSIDE THE TRASK BUILDING
May 24, 2019 | 11:35 a.m.
The carnage begins

The sound of glass shattering was surprisingly subdued. During post-incident interviews with the police, people working in offices near the lobby say they barely heard anything. The heavy carpet in the entryway probably absorbed some of the sound, as did the building's sound-absorbing acoustics, giving a macabre meaning to "deadly silence."

Wilson's desk crumbled into firewood as the SUV rammed it. If the weight of the SUV wasn't enough to do Wilson in, then the wood shards from his desk spearing him in the chest surely killed him. The woman whose audible gasp caught Wilson's attention was already running by the time he noticed; she had managed to evade being hit by the SUV. She ran quietly, a scream of terror emerging only after a few more seconds passed. Her silence gave

Tomlinson time to emerge from the vehicle, gather the two weapons, the extra ammunition, and the ski mask he had brought with him. He pulled the mask over his head, stuffed the additional ammunition in the pockets of the Army surplus coat he was wearing, held the Glock in his right hand and the shotgun in his left, and started walking, first past offices on that floor then toward the open-air staircase in the lobby that led to the top floor.

He aimed each weapon—pointed them is a more accurate way of saying it—in the direction of any movement he sensed, like the woman who was running from the security desk. He raised the Glock and squeezed the trigger five or six times, firing rounds in her direction. One round hit her in the back of her head. She dropped as silently as she ran, dead before she crumbled.

Tomlinson slung the shotgun over his right shoulder and walked down the hallways of the building's middle floor past the cubicle farms—Trask called them team centers. There was a small conference room connected to each of these team centers. He pointed the weapons in opposite directions, pulling off one round after another as he traveled. As he fired, people scattered. Not so much yelling, although there was a fair share of "Run!" "What?" "Wait, NO!" as people scurried behind and under desks.

Soon Tomlinson's walk turned into a slow jog. He quickly moved down one hallway on the middle floor and ascended the open-air stairwell to the top level. As he continued to shoot, he could hear a cacophony of sounds from the people inside. One woman was yelling, "There's a guy with a gun, and he's shooting the place up!" That prompted Mel to assume a faster jog to accelerate his movement. *Gotta cover more ground!*

At first, Trask International employees on the upper floor paid little or no attention to the commotion and carnage that was unfolding downstairs because they didn't associate gunfire with the sounds and noises emitting from the lower floor. A construction project was underway in the lower levels of the building and some of the construction crew used nail guns to install studding for new meeting rooms, so a loud and rapid "bang-bang" sound was by some considered little more than background noise.

Joe Barron heard the sound, and he too thought it was a nail gun. He was on the second floor, standing by coworker Steve Donelson's cubicle, engaged in a work/not work conversation. They were two of the three P.R. professionals who work in the Trask International building. A third, manager Burt Schorr, was on vacation that day. Lucky guy.

Barron heard the rapid banging sound, but like so many, he thought it was the nail gun.

"Wait, what's that noise?" Donelson asked. His question was barely finished when the sound of Dorothy Miller, the administrative assistant who worked with Barron and Donelson, took over his senses.

"JOE, THERE'S A GUY WITH A GUN, AND HE'S SHOOTING THE PLACE UP!" Miller screamed. She was in her early 60s with a low-key personality and was screaming at the top of her lungs and running as fast as she could.

Barron didn't see the gunman, but the fear in Miller's voice, the wide-eyed expression on her face, and the fact she was *running* told him something was very wrong. As she approached, he realized the "bang-bang" sound he was hearing kept getting closer. It became obvious; man + gun + Dorothy running + sound getting very close = a guy is shooting, and he is going to be here any second.

"HIDE! Get under a desk!" Barron shouted.

Everyone dove under a desk.

The same desk. Five people. Mostly in front of it rather than under it. It was one of several desks situated in the nearest team center. The desk near a bulletin board holding a "RUN, HIDE,

FIGHT" active shooter advice poster corporate human resources had distributed a few months ago.

"Try the other desk!" someone yelled.

All five individuals ran to the next desk. It would have been comical if the rapid-fire sounds of Tomlinson's guns weren't ripping through the air.

That's when Barron saw the law library, a larger conference room with a solid metal door. A door with a lock on it.

"The library. GO!!"

Barron reached the library doorway first. He stood by the doorway watching the others run toward him.

I should be looking for the guy who's shooting, he thought.

Geez, I didn't know Dorothy could run so fast.

Barron, why are you thinking about that, for chrissakes?

Once everyone was inside, Barron slammed the door shut and threw the deadbolt to lock the door. Everyone dove under the conference table in the center of the room. A room with no windows. A room with bookshelves lining the walls. There was no way to see if the crazy gunman was outside. For those in that small room, a waiting in terror game had begun.

MONTGOMERY COUNTY POLICE
May 24, 2019 | 11:40 a.m.
911 DISPATCH

Dispatcher: "911, what is your emergency?"

Caller: "I'm at the Trask building on Udell Road, and there is someone inside shooting off a gun!"

Dispatcher: "OK, you are at the Trask building?"

Caller: "Yes, 1041 Udell Road. Please hurry!"

Dispatcher: "You said there is someone shooting a gun?"

Caller: "Yes!"

Dispatcher: "Is anyone shot?"

Caller: "I think so. I don't know for sure."

Dispatcher: "OK, are you in a secure location?"

Caller: "I think so."

Dispatcher: "What is your name, sir?"

Caller: "Tom Larry. I can hear the guy shooting."

Dispatcher: "It's a man?"

Caller: "OK, I don't know that for sure."

Dispatcher: "That's all right. Please stay where you are. Help is on the way. Is anyone else near you?"

Caller: "I think so. There's a woman behind a desk near me."

The dispatcher heard Larry's voice raise as he shouted, "Suzy, are you OK?"

Dispatcher: "Sir, please don't shout. If there is a shooter nearby, they may hear you, OK?"

Caller: "OK, yeah."

After finishing the call, the dispatcher turned to another channel. "Standby. Active shooter. 1041 Udell Road, Bethesda. Repeat, active shooter. 1041 Udell Road, Bethesda. Nearest units please respond. We are looking at the Rust Bucket on Udell Road in Bethesda."

At this point, Brenda Connor, the Public Information Officer for the Montgomery County Police Department, tapped a few keys on her laptop and sent out the following tweet:

> @MontCoPolice
> **Police are responding to calls from 1041 Udell Road. Reports of an active shooter. Please avoid the area.**
> 11:45 a.m. - May 24, 2019

Then another:

> @MontCoPolice
> **Alert #NewsMedia, please stand by for details.**
> 11:47 a.m. - May 24, 2019

And a third:

> @MontCoPolice
> **General public, please refrain from calling the MontCo Police for updates. We will provide details via social media as they become available.**
> 11:51 a.m. - May 24, 2019

Conner only had to add the address to her first tweet. The rest of the message had been prepared in advance. *Thank God for advance planning*, she thought.

CRISIS LIFE CYCLE
STEP ONE—IDENTIFY AND NOTIFY

TWO HOURS AWAY FROM THE TRASK BUILDING
HIGHWAY 50 - EAST OF ANNAPOLIS, MARYLAND
May 24, 2019 | 11:59 a.m.

Bert Schorr was the manager of Trask International's regional public relations office in Bethesda. He was unaware of the carnage going on since he was driving to his weekend home on Maryland's Eastern Shore. His lazy gaze upon the highway and surroundings was broken when he turned on his car radio to catch the noon news and heard the following:

"Police in Bethesda are responding to reports of an active shooter at 1041 Udell Road."

Wait, what?

"... reports are there are multiple serious injuries, possible fatalities."

That's my office!

"We are efforting to learn more about what is happening in this Trask facility. This is Marc Tilling reporting for WDCN."

There's that word I hate: FACILITY. It doesn't mean what you think. Wait, why am I thinking this now? What's up with Joe, Steve, Dorothy, and the team?? Gotta call them.

He could feel his pulse speeding up as he looked for a place to pull over. *Don't rush! You make mistakes when you rush. Any point on the side of Highway 50 will have to do.* He threw on the blinkers on his car, grabbed his phone, and said, "Hey Siri, call the office."

As he waited for the connection, his mind raced. *And 'efforting?' They verbed a noun. Jesus, Schorr, Steve Donelson's bad habits are wearing off on you.*

There was no answer.

"Siri, call Joe."

Siri obeyed, calling Joe's office line, not his cell phone.

Barron's office phone rang. No answer. In the excitement of the moment, Schorr didn't think to call anyone's smartphone.

"Siri, call Dorothy." Dorothy's desk number was different from Schorr's office.

No answer.

Jesus Christ, what is going on?

In haste he kept asking Siri to call the office rather than cell phones. No one was at their desks. Schorr panicked after not reaching anyone's mobile phone and didn't think to call a landline.

He next asked Siri to call Ed Reisman, his manager, who works in Foot, a small town in Westchester County, New York. Reisman answered on the first ring.

"Bert? Aren't you supposed to be on vacation today?"

"Ed, I just heard on the radio about something bad going down at Bethesda."

"What?"

"An active shooter. A gunman. Shooting live rounds."

"What?"

"Ed, do I really need to repeat that?"

"Wait, what? Never mind. Bert, what's happening?"

Schorr provided what little information he had, adding that he was unable to reach anyone on his immediate team.

"OK, Bert, where are you now?"

"On the side of Highway 50, just outside of Annapolis."

"What's closer for you? Bethesda or your shore house?"

"Shore house, but I'm turning around right now."

"OK, let me see what I can find out. Don't try going into the building once you get there."

"Yeah, right Ed." He ended the call and pulled into traffic as soon as there was an opening. *Are U-turns legal in Maryland? Probably not.*

He tried one more phone number before he pulled back into traffic. Dorothy Miller's personal phone, which was left behind at her desk in her pocketbook. He didn't try another number. He turned his car around and hit the gas.

Back in Foot, Reisman quickly thumbed through his contacts. He needed a specific part of his network. Big companies with operations spread across wide geographies need networks. Not just the electronic networks that connect us all, but networks of eyes and ears on the ground. Someone who is in the know when no one else is. And having contacts with law enforcement is especially helpful when the wrong situation occurs. Ed Reisman punched in a phone number. The recipient answered right away.

"Ed?" Hello is a dead word anymore for most people using smartphones. You already know who's calling.

"Frank, yeah. Is something happening in Bethesda?"

Frank Reardon was a retired Maryland state trooper who spent his spare time doing investigations for a district attorney and some litigation attorneys.

"I heard something about an active shooter. Is it at one of your offices?"

"That's what I'm hearing, yeah. Can you confirm this, Frank? If what I hear is happening, then it's pretty serious."

"Let me make some calls and get back to you."

"As quick as you can, Frank. We can't reach anyone who works in that building."

"Understood. Give me the address, so I'm talking about the right active shooter situation." That last line was half joking, half serious.

Finishing his call with Reisman, Reardon next made a call to the Montgomery County Police Department and briefly talked to a very harried sounding Brenda Connor. *That's all I need. Confirmation.* He sent the following text to Reisman:

> "It's happening, Ed. Undetermined number of shooters. May only be one. People trapped inside at the Udell Road address."

INSIDE THE TRASK BUILDING
May 24, 2019 | 11:48 a.m.

Just 50 feet down the hall from where Barron and company were hiding, Ted Lewiston was waiting in terror by himself. He heard the gunfire and a woman screaming, then flipped over a desk and crawled behind it, pulling several office chairs around him to create a makeshift shelter. He prayed as he shivered. Gunshots and screams interrupted his whispers.

"Our father, who art in heaven, hallowed be . . ."

POW, POW, POW!

". . . hallowed be thy name. Thy kingdom . . ."

POW! POW! "Ahhh, no, stop . . ."

". . . thy kingdom come, on Earth, as it is in heaven."

POWPOWPOWPOW

". . . give us this day our daily bread, and forgive us . . ."

POWPOWPOW

". . . and forgive us our trespasses, as we forgive . . ."

POWPOWPOWPOW

". . . as we forgive those who trespass against us . . ."

He was holding a chair to provide some cover for himself as he hid beneath the desk. But as the shooting persisted his hands began to shake so badly that the chair was loudly rattling. He let go of the chair and wrapped his arms around himself as he continued to pray. He thought of his wife and his two girls as tears rolled down his cheeks.

Ted Lewiston was far from the only person immersed in tearful prayer at that moment. Others were immersed in more forceful actions.

Elsewhere in the building, and well within earshot of Tomlinson's gunfire, Becca Santini, director of IT for the Bethesda Trask office, was huddled beneath the desk in her office. Her administrative assistant, Jonathan Osipow, was with her. Osipow, a thin young man of 22 years, was shaking like a puppy on its first visit to the veterinarian's office. Like Lewiston, he was quietly saying a prayer.

Santini put her hand on Osipow's shoulder and whispered, "It's OK to be scared Jonathan, but we are going to be all right."

Osipow looked at Santini and started to ask how she knew that when gunshots again interrupted him. He wrapped his arms tightly around his legs, stuck in a fetal position beneath Santini's desk.

Santini knew what her coworker was about to ask.

"I know it because we are getting out of here. Right. Now."

She rose to a crouched position and moved across her office toward a credenza that sat opposite her desk. Atop the credenza, seated on a custom-made ceramic base, was a 20-pound shot put.

At five feet nine inches tall, Santini was close to the same shape she was when she was a member of the track and field squad at Towson University in Towson, Maryland. At least she told herself she was close to being in the same shape.

She didn't run on the track and field team; she threw the shot put. The ball she threw in competition weighed 13 pounds, but she trained with this 20-pound version her father, a tool and die maker, fashioned for her at his shipping depot in Baltimore.

Placing the shot put in the palm of her right hand, Santini lifted the solid metal sphere to her shoulder, right beneath her right jawline. *It's been a minute, Becca. You can do this*, she said to herself, forgetting how heavy this training shot put was.

She raised herself to the semi-squatting position shot put throwers use (she hated it when her friends who weren't involved with track and field called her a "shot putter"). Her left knee was bent, supporting her weight. Her right leg situated behind her also bent, but in a position to launch herself forward. She envisioned her coach telling her, "Get low, Becca, crouch then spin and lunge."

Santini heard gunshots. They sounded like they were just feet down the hallway from her office. Osipow winced at the sound.

Do it NOW, she screamed to herself.

Santini spun once and vaulted the shot put directly toward the window of her office. She was on the first floor, and it was less than a 10-foot drop from her window to the ground outside. Osipow gasped.

The window didn't break.

But it did crack. A spider-web pattern of cracks about three times the size of the shot put.

Santini was panting from the exertion. It had been nearly 20 years since she was in competition. "Gimme a minute, Jonathan," she said, readying to catch her breath and try it again.

"No, Mrs. Santini. We ARE leaving now," she heard Osipow say, looking up to see him picking up the shot put, raising it above his head with both hands, then launching it for a second time at the window.

This time the metal sphere went through the window. The glass made more of a muffled cracking sound than the typical shatter one would expect. Nevertheless, the end result almost immediately got the attention of the police who were outside of her office.

Outside the building, the police heard, then saw the miniature explosion of glass. They next saw two individuals climbing out of the broken window and dropping to the ground. Immediately four S.W.A.T. officers were right next to Santini and Osipow before they could get to their feet.

"Show me your hands, now!" one officer screamed. His service revolver was pointed at the two.

"Cool your jets, Crockett and Tubbs. We work here," said Santini, pointing at the building with her thumb. She was looking at her arm, which received a cut as she jumped out of the window. Fortunately, some heavy bushes helped break her and Osipow's fall.

"My partner said show me your hands!" another officer yelled.

"Here they are, Wiggum," Santini said, referring to the police chief on "The Simpsons" as she held up her hands. Osipow did the same.

"We don't need an attitude, lady," the cop she identified as Wiggum said.

"And as of right now I don't need guns shot or pointed in my face. So, there we are."

The fourth S.W.A.T. member looked at the 20-pound shot put, then at Santini. "Did you use that to break the window?"

"Man, Columbo, nothing gets past you, does it?"

The four officers led Santini and Osipow away, toward a medical van.

"What WAS that thing you used to break the window?" Wiggum asked Santini.

"My ex-boyfriend's left nut."

Before Wiggum could speak Osipow chimed in. "Mrs. Santini used to throw the shot put for her college cross country team."

"Track and field, Jonathan. But, yeah, that was me."

CRISIS LIFE CYCLE
STEP TWO—ACTIVATE THE COMMUNICATIONS RESPONSE TEAM

TRASK HEADQUARTERS
May 24, 2019 | 12:01 p.m.

Reisman took a moment to take in Reardon's message confirming the shooting was going on, then sent emergency text messages to Alexis Shimada, Trask International's director of human resources, and Ron Reynolds, Trask International's chief legal counsel. The three of them comprised Trask International's crisis response team. "Guys, we have a crisis. I have confirmed it, and it's a big one," Reisman said. "Need to get the wheels moving immediately."

Next, he sent a message via Slack to Geeta Allen, senior communications specialist for Trask International.

> "Geeta, come see me stat. Something bad is going down in Bethesda."

Within minutes Reisman had briefed Allen. She returned to her laptop and sent out the first of multiple messages:

Internal statement from Trask, Inc., delivered via Slack, posted at 12:05 p.m. on May 24, 2019, by Geeta Allen, a senior communications specialist for Trask charged with handling all first-line press inquiries.

> "Trask International is aware of a shooting situation at our office building at 1041 Udell Road, Bethesda, Maryland. We are working with the local police, who are the primary source of information about the incident. At this time, we ask employees not to try and contact anyone they may know at that site as it may negatively compromise the police operation."

Next, Allen opened another document on her laptop, read it carefully before cutting and pasting it into her Trask International Twitter account.

@TraskIntl
Trask International is aware of an active shooter situation at the Udell Road office building in Bethesda, MD. We are working with local police, who are the primary source of information about the incident.
12:07 p.m. - May 24, 2019

She hit send and looked at the "likes" and "retweets" button under the statement. The heart-shaped "like" icon was pulsing, doing its version of a digital heartbeat. Both icons were blinking and the numbers next to them rose sharply. "Twitter is exploding over this," she muttered.

Allen sent a Slack message to John Taylor, her immediate supervisor. "John, the announcements are out."

Taylor got up from his desk – he sat less than 20 feet from Allen - walked over to her desk and said, "That's fine, Geeta. Keep monitoring any activity. We're watching this on Sprout Social, right?"

CRISIS LIFE CYCLE
STEP THREE—GATHER THE FACTS

"Sprout Social, Hootsuite, the works," Allen said. Subscriptions to social media monitoring tools can be expensive, but in cases like an active shooter crisis they are also vitally important and pay for themselves in no time. Knowing who is saying what about a situation can help a company react and/or pivot depending on what is being said or what is happening, they provide lifesaving information to authorities, and they help maintain contact with customers.

Sprout Social and Hootsuite monitor and flag any social media chatter that mentions Trask. Of course, an age old saying about technology—garbage in/garbage out—still applied. Monitoring tools can only look for what you tell them to find. If you ask Hootsuite to follow news about a shooting on Main Street, but the activity is taking place on Madison Avenue, then you get bad data. The trick is knowing what to ask for and how to separate the clutter.

Clutter should be the alter ego of social media, particularly Twitter. A Pew Research study from 2018 determined that an overwhelming majority of tweets are generated by "bots," or automated software systems designed to generate or retweet Twitter activity per specific subject[1]. Most suspect that a lot of political tweets are generated by bots, but the business world is also becoming increasingly sophisticated in using bots. A flow of tweets about a specific subject can generate responses and retweets from real people; savvy marketers can use the retweets and original messages to formulate marketing plans that enable them to "serve" specific messages[2] to audiences.

Some researchers call this the rage marketing machine, and to an extent it works. If there is enough social media activity surrounding a specific topic, then marketing plans can be adjusted, political agendas can be rewritten. Indeed, social media in 2019 can accomplish far more than getting *Saturday Night Live* to hire Betty White as a host.

The marketing of rage is a double-edged sword for sure. Rage can be a powerful marketing emotion, and there is no shortage of technology advisers who can show how an industry can exploit mortification for profit. To be sure, rage associated with the loss of human life is a risky mix for marketers. No one is going to try to sell stain remover in the aftermath of a mass shooting. At least not yet. But they are going to pull on some heartstrings regarding political activity surrounding gun control.

Probably not going to get a lot of anger tweets from the competition, Allen thought.

Allen added a few more search terms: Udell Road, Udel Road (for those who cannot read maps or spell), Trask shooter, Trask, and gun control. The objective is to keep atop what is being said about what's happening in Bethesda. This was the type of planning and organizing Allen excelled at.

Allen had some additional tools to help her with that challenge. To get some real world/real time data, Allen turned to another online resource called Answer the Public, a social media and search monitoring source that provides insights into what people are searching for online. Answer the Public is a website that helps make sense of the nearly three billion Google searches that take place every day ... everything from kickstarting a jammed printer to how much the President of the United States earns. For a business, this is a priceless resource that tells Allen exactly what Trask audiences are asking. Answer the Public provides a "Who," "What," "Where," "When," and "Why" of what people are going online to search for. It provides insights in plain English.

Going straight to the search bar, Allen entered "Trask Bethesda" and hit the enter key. The results took about 30 seconds to come back, but the insights from the tweets were timeless.

"What is going on at Trask Bethesda?"

"Where is the Trask building in Bethesda?"

"How many people work at the Trask site in Bethesda?"

"Is the shooting at all Trask offices?"

"Does Laney Tolliver work at Trask Bethesda?"

Who the heck is Laney Tolliver? thought Allen, who did a quick name search in the company directory and determined that there is no such person in Bethesda, or elsewhere, on Trask International's payroll. The tweets from her research continued.

Where is the Trask building in Bethesda?

Where is Udell Avenue?

Where is Udell Lane?

I told my congressman I wanted better gun control laws.

This is what happens when you try to control guns. For every action . . .

Yes, the world would be MUCH safer if everyone had a loaded gun at their side.

The Second Amendment has to be amended to get these weapons of war off the streets. It was written back when they used muskets and cannons. It is not appropriate for today's sick, violent world.

Riiiight. So if someone is trying to steal my car should I load my fucking musket?

The Second Amendment was written when people had common sense.

How do you expect gun control to be effective when criminals obtain guns through illegal means? Criminals and mass shooters will not hand over their guns just because you passed a law. Gun control makes no sense at all. People like you and I are not the problem.

When was the last time that any part of the Bill of Rights was changed? Not since 1787, right?

No, ace. It was changed in the 1920s to give women the right to vote.

Welp, that's another topic for discussion, isn't it? LOL

You're an asshole.

The debate raged on. *Are these people even INTERESTED in what's happening in Bethesda?* Allen wondered. For now, though, her job was to see what, if anything, is being said about Trask International, Inc. There were only a few tweets mentioning the company specifically.

Who'd @TraskIntl fire?

Somebody with @TraskIntl didn't like their commission, huh?

No bother. @TraskIntl is a horrible company.

That last tweet generated its own share of blowback. *Probably people who work for the company. Next thing you know Trask will be accused of "planting" responses on social media.*

One of the subcategories Answer the Public provides is displaying how the topic you search for compares to others. When Allen searched "Trask Shooting Bethesda" for comparison, the following came back:

"Is this another Bakersfield truck stop?"
"Trask Bethesda and Rite Aid Aberdeen Maryland"
"Trask Bethesda and Mercy Hospital Chicago"
"Trask Bethesda and yoga studio Tallahassee."

The results mentioned situations where mass shootings took place at businesses. Allen did a Wikipedia search to have background notes. The incidents included a September 20, 2018 shooting at a Rite Aid distribution center in Aberdeen, Maryland, where four people were shot and killed; a November 19, 2018 shooting at Mercy Hospital in Chicago, where someone's ex-fiancé showed up and shot her, an attending physician, a pharmacist, and a cop. THAT one ended when police killed the shooter in a brief but violent shootout. *Trying not to think of that one much,* Allen said to herself.

The other two shootings that were mentioned included a November 2, 2018 shooting at a hot yoga studio in Tallahassee, Florida where a gunman showed up, shot and killed two employees, shot four others, and pistol whipped a seventh person before turning the gun on himself. Last mentioned was a September 11, 2018 shooting at T&T Trucking in Bakersfield, California, where six people died.

They're comparing us to other businesses that had mass shootings. Not surprising. Gun control lobby will want to build a case, and the Second Amendment gang will want their own defense. Ok, one more search. Allen clicked on the heading "Related" and held her breath. *Here is where the bad stuff shows up,* she thought.

"Is Trask's CEO an NRA member?"

"What political candidates does Trask support?"

"Do Republicans or Democrats comprise most of Trask's Board of Directors?"

In the absence of facts, the people will make up their own stories. Allen remembered that line from one of her public relations professors at Syracuse University. The "Related" searches are the place where the homegrown stories are often cultivated.

She gathered this insight, especially the "Related" search terms, and put them into a spreadsheet for her supervisor to share with Ed Reisman, who was reviewing Allen's social media research when his phone rang. It was Ron Reynolds in legal, responding to his messages from earlier.

"Ed, are you SURE about what's happening in Bethesda?"

"Yes, Ron, I'm sure. And hi. I'm fine. How are you?"

"Sorry. This is coming at me pretty fast."

"Remember the crisis planning, Ron. It will all come at us faster than we can imagine. And, yes, I called the Montgomery County Police Department to confirm this is all happening in real time. They are tweeting about it, too."

Reynolds was quiet for a moment. "Tweeting? Like what we were working on?"

"Yep."

"Guess I owe you an apology for being such a jerk that day." He was referring to his demeanor months ago when Reisman strong-armed Reynolds and several other Trask executives into a crisis communications planning seminar. Reynolds was particularly reluctant to participate.

"You? A jerk? C'mon, Ron."

"Ha. Are we notifying customers?"

"Via channels we discussed, yes."

After the call, Reisman decided to dial one other number. Inside the Rust Bucket, Joe Barron's phone buzzed.

"Ed?"

"Joe, yes it's me. Where are you?"

"Law library conference room, around the corner from our team center."

"Are you with anyone?"

"Me, Steve, Dorothy, and a temp. Sorry, can't recall the name in these circumstances. Ed, what's happening out there?"

"I don't have a lot of information, Joe. But I know there is an active shooter in the building and . . ."

Right then the conversation was interrupted by loud and nearby gunshots. Barron dropped his phone and Reisman nearly leapt from his chair.

"Ed, I can't stay on the phone."

"I know. Be safe. Help IS on the way."

"Thanks, Ed."

Afraid that the shooter could be nearby, everyone kept their use of their phones to a minimum lest the bad guy hears voices. Some made calls, but kept their voices to a low murmur.

CRISIS LIFE CYCLE
STEP FOUR—FORMULATE THE RESPONSE

Twitter message from Trask International Customer Relations
May 24, 2019 | 12:15 p.m.

@TraskIntlCustRel

1/2 Sad news. There is an active shooter situation under-way at our offices in Bethesda, Maryland. Please keep our staff in your thoughts and prayers.

@TraskIntlCustRel

2/2 We know shots were fired and people trapped in the building. We are cooperating with the police as the situation unfolds.

Third tweet. Sent five minutes later.

@TraskIntlCustRel

Please steer clear of the Trask Int'l building at 1041 Udell Road, Bethesda. Police are on site. It is not a safe environment right now.

Fourth tweet. Sent two minutes later.

@TraskIntlCustRel

We are furloughing all bots in our customer service phone lines, replacing them with real people. Yep, for a limited time you can talk to someone rather than drilling your way through a telephone menu.

The prepared in advance version of the last tweet included instructions to include a "yaaay" avatar. The individual managing this Twitter account made the smart decision to ignore that piece of advice.

This tweet was repeated on Facebook, using multiple "yay" avatars. That avatar was reused for multiple customer outreach efforts.

The Slack message arrived for Odemis Salazar, Michael Wayne, and Meaghan O'Halloran. All three were internal customer service representatives for Trask International. Located in the headquarters building in the New York suburbs and the operations there were focused on training sessions for remote server operations.

"Emergency protocols are in place," the message began. "Switch to manual telephone response until further notice."

"Ugh, what's up," Wayne said.

"A crisis of some kind, what else," Salazar answered without looking at her coworker.

"I just saw the Tweet. We're going to be answering phones for the foreseeable future. Shit," Wayne said. "Why do we have to do this?"

"Because there is a man with a gun killing people at our offices in Bethesda, that's why," the answer came directly from Sylvester Moore, Trask's senior vice president of marketing. "I was coming over this way to make sure you three had the message and see if you had any questions."

"Oh," Salazar said.

"I can tell from your response that you got the message and had at least one question," Moore continued. "Anybody else got a question? We're not being shot at, so I have lots of time to answer." Moore was never one to suffer fools gladly. He certainly was not going to start now.

"I think my colleague was just concerned about the volume of calls we may get," Salazar said.

"I get it," Moore said, looking around and seeing an empty desk. "Is that phone connected to the customer service network?"

"Yes. Why?" O'Halloran said.

Moore said nothing and simply took a seat at the empty desk. By coincidence the phone at that desk rang first. "Trask International customer service, Sylvester speaking, how may I help you?" The three listened as Moore conducted his phone conversation.

"Yes sir. Thank you, sir. If it is OK, may I ask your sales representative to reach out to you via telephone? Thank you."

He took notes as he talked, promising he would have someone call them back before the close of business.

O'Halloran, Wayne, and Salazar were all at a loss for words. Moore looked at the three of them, then spoke.

"We are in a crisis, people, so we all chip in, right? I don't ask you to do anything I wouldn't do myself. I can't stay here long, but I do plan to stay as long as I can." Then looking straight at Wayne, "Michael, I think your phone is ringing."

Wayne, embarrassed beyond words, sheepishly picked up his phone and went to work.

CRISIS LIFE CYCLE
STEP FIVE—IDENTIFY THE STAKEHOLDERS

ED REISMAN'S OFFICE
Phone call with Ron Reynolds

"OK, Ed, I should let you go for now. But I'll be in touch."

"Wait, there is a 'to do' for you."

"What's that?"

"How many members of the board are also American Handgun Association members?"

"What? Why?"

"Because people are already searching online for that information. Considering we are in the midst of a possible mass shooting, then we may want to think about covering our flanks."

Reynolds was quiet for a moment before speaking. "I can't tell our board members what organizations they can or can't join, Ed."

"I'm not asking you to do that. Just suggesting we be aware of who is a member. Let me know so that we can adjust some of the contingency Q&As we have."

"What do you propose we say? 'We're asking board member so and so to renounce his AHA membership?'"

"Again, no. But we want to be prepared to say the members of our board have the right to join any organization, but that said memberships do not speak for Trask International."

Another, momentary silence. "That may be a tough one for some members of the board to swallow."

"One, they don't have to like it. Two, it's Trask International we are watching out for. And one other thing."

"What?"

"What PACs has Trask International donated to?"

"Why … oh, I get it. In case our political donations come back to bite us."

"Exactly."

"Crisis planning IS a big iceberg, isn't it?"

"It's just like we talked about, Ron. Thank you for your help here."

"Thank me once I haven't been beheaded by the CEO."

"I hear he takes small bites. You'll be ok."

As the call ended, Reisman pulled up the Q&A set that was prepared months in advance of today's events. He selected a random spot midway down the list of questions and began typing:

Question: Is it true that (NAME) on your board of directors is a member of the American Handgun Association?

Answer: We don't closely follow the outside interests of all our board members.

Follow-up Question: We know (NAME) is an AHA member. Why don't you?

Follow Answer: I never said we did not know. I only said this subject falls outside of our purview.

Question: I understand Trask donated to the (PAC NAME), which actively supports gun rights. Is that why you donated to that PAC?

Answer: We invested in PAC NAME because its interests were aligned with our goals to grow the business and create equity for our stakeholders.

Reisman made a note: *That answer needs work. We need to show we invested because it not only helps our bottom line, but it also helps make the world a better place. Yeah, better place … one where everyone can carry a gun. Yeah, this is going to need some work. But it's a start.*

Back over at Geeta Allen's desk, she gave some of the Answer the Public data to her intern to add additional search terms to

Trask's Sprout Social and Hootsuite accounts.

The intern then set up a monitoring page on Hootsuite, using some of the search terms Allen identified. This gives Trask a real-time look at what people were saying and what they did with the information.

It will take her a few minutes to set that up, Allen thought. She started glancing at the messages she had just sent out to see what the response is on Twitter when the thought occurred to her:

Shit, Joe Barron works in Bethesda! Can I get him on the phone?

Barron's cell phone buzzed. He hated the array of ring tones that are available, so he always kept it on silent. He pulled it from his pocket to look at it. He knew everyone was avoiding phone conversations, but this call was from Geeta Allen. He swiped with his thumb to answer.

"Joe?"

"I'm here, Geeta. It's not a good time. I talked to Ed a few minutes ago."

"I know it's a bad time." She didn't know Barron had already talked to Reisman. "Joe, are you OK?"

"For now, yeah. A bunch of us are holed up in a conference room."

Barron was whispering. He could sense Donelson and Miller giving him side eye. Allen spoke next.

"OK, be careful, will you?"

"I will, buddy. I promise."

"You owe me another dinner, Barron."

"I'll make good. Promise."

He tapped the phone to end the call. The group had been in the room for some time, and the silence was getting to everyone. Barron saw Donelson looking at him.

"Ed again?" Donelson said.

"No, someone I know at corporate headquarters."

Donelson kept looking at Barron.

"Stop it, Steve. She's just a friend."

"Yes, stop it," Miller chimed in in a hushed voice. "This isn't high school."

"Speaking of high school," Donelson said with a moment of realization. "Local schools may let out soon. Wonder if they know what's going on."

"According to Twitter, they already do," said Janet, the temp who was helping. She hadn't been talking but was intently focused on her phone.

"Anyone looking out of the window is going to see it's more than Andy Taylor and Barney Fife outside in the parking lot," Donelson said, referring to the old television show, *The Andy Griffith Show* where the two main characters were Sheriff Andy Taylor and Deputy Barney Fife.

"Everybody is affected by this. One way or another," Miller said.

CRISIS LIFE CYCLE
STEP ONE (AGAIN)—IDENTIFY AND NOTIFY

AMERICAN HANDGUN ASSOCIATION HEADQUARTERS*
FAIRFAX VIRGINIA
May 24, 2019 | 11:56 a.m.

"Delvin, have you seen the news? Shooting at an office building in Bethesda."

Delvin Constantine looked up from his desk to see his colleague Linda Daynard at the door.

"What shooting, Linda?"

"An office building in Bethesda. Not sure how many have been shot but over 100 persons are trapped inside. Initial news reports say it may be a lone shooter. Not much other information is available right now."

---

*This conversation is based on a recording from the National Rifle Association headquarters on April 30, 1999, where NRA leaders discussed the mass shooting at Columbine High School. It was reported by National Public Radio on November 9, 2021.

Constantine sat back and took a deep breath.

Daynard wanted to push for some action by the organization. "Should we have our social media at the ready to shoot down the haters?"

"Linda, everything we do here has a potential downside. Let's not kid ourselves about being macho and showing how damn tough we can be in the face of yet another potential black eye. Do we know anything more than what's on the television?"

"There is some speculation that it is a former employee of the company."

"What company, by the way?"

"Trask International. They do cloud consulting or something like that."

"So, it's not some hillbilly or fruitcake who is involved . . ."

"Doesn't look that way."

"But we have hillbillies and fruitcakes on our member rolls, and they can always go off on some tangent."

"That's already happening," Daynard said. "Twitter is, as the saying goes, exploding. Pro and anti-gun rhetoric statements running wild."

Constantine shrugged. "That just demonstrates the free speech aspect of social media. Anyone can say whatever they want. And I suspect more than a few are bots. What's the research show? More than half of the rage tweets are generated by bots? We can't do much about that. So, for now, let's just keep monitoring what people are saying. We have a way to do that, don't we?"

"Yes, it's a tool called Answer the Public and it tells us exactly what people are using as search terms."

Constantine smiled. "It's fun living in the future."

"Delvin, there is one other thing to consider."

"What?"

"Timing. If anyone has been killed—and reports from TV say that's a distinct possibility—then someone will be burying a loved one right when we're having regional conferences. Do we want to consider rescheduling something?"

Constantine didn't need a minute to think about it. "No. Sadly there is some kind of shooting almost every day. Call it the price of a free society, if you will, but we can't reschedule everything we do around a family burial or any other event. I know that's harsh, but it's the path we need to take."

Daynard was quiet, then muttered, "That's a horrible juxtaposition."

"Agreed, but it is the best of a lot of very bad options."

"So, we go on with our lives?"

"Business as usual."

Daynard was about to leave when Constantine spoke. "Do we have any meetings coming up with members of Congress from Maryland or elsewhere?"

Daynard tapped on her iPad then responded, "Yes, we have a briefing with Senator Pratt from Maryland next week."

Constantine's brow furrowed. "That's OK, he likes to say we 'invest in his agenda,'³ so let's hold that for now but keep an eye on his office and what, if anything, he says." Daynard nodded, then left.

The American Handgun Association would continue to stand back and react . . . but only when prompted.

SHOUTING ON TWITTER. OR, IS ANYONE LISTENING?

Tweets from @GooseGoslinHighSchool
May 24, 2019 | 11:58 a.m.

> Montgomery County police are responding to a situation reported at an office building adjacent to our campus. Details are unconfirmed, but as a precaution we are under a soft lockdown at this time.

> @GooseGoslinHighSchool
> Students & personnel are safe/out of harm's way. The police activity is taking place approx. 1 mile from the campus. The soft lockdown is an abundance of caution move. Please await further instructions before driving to the school.

> @GooseGoslinHighSchool
> Again, this is only for the campus of Goslin High. Further official information will come through his account only.

The tweets above were a part of the Montgomery County School District's crisis communications plan. They were developed after lengthy discussions with staff and faculty. This was the moment when the question, "Is anyone listening?" would be answered.

PRIVATE HOME
COCKEREL DRIVE, BETHESDA, MARYLAND
May 24, 2019 | Noon

Freelance writer Tony Madden was in his home office catching up on episodes of *The Flight Attendant* on HBO Max when his phone pinged. It was a Twitter message from the Montgomery County School District telling him that for safety reasons the building will be in lockdown.

Cool, Madden thought. *First, Kaley Cuoco, then a couple reruns of The Blacklist before the kids come home.* Callous? Perhaps, but some thirty-plus years of mass shootings and violence in the streets has imbued him and many others to what otherwise may be the natural human emotion of fret and worry.

Madden was more sanguine than some. There was no shortage of blowback over the Twitter messages from the police. The responses came over the Twittersphere like locusts.

The online shouting just continued, unabated and becoming even more intense as more people chime in.

> @BethesdaBeth
> A "soft lockdown"? WTF does that even mean?

> @MDAMom
> This is what happens when we don't have good gun laws.

> @DemandGunLawLarry
> Maybe something will be done about gun violence now that corporate America (sic) has been dragged into the conversation.

> @AHA_Respect
> Guys, can we let this settle down before putting anyone, or any business, on trial?

> @FedEx
> We are aware of the incident playing out on Udell Road in Bethesda, and we are temporarily suspending deliveries to the Independence Boulevard corridor.

@ToMakeItClear
Hey @TraskIntl, in 2018 you donated millions to Republican candidates and lobbying groups.

@NRA_Respect
Hey @ToMakeItClear, this isn't the time.

@MDAMom
@NRA_Respect. Not the time??? Let me know when it is.

The social media shouting match continued, unabated, for the rest of the day and well into the next day. Geeta Allen's monitoring flagged tweets like the one asking how much Trask International donated to gun lobby PACs, and she shared that insight with Reisman, who could use that in his back pocket when dealing with press inquiries. Each time someone connected Trask International to a PAC, to the AHA, or other controversial subject, she would flag that tweet and forward it to Reisman. Fortunately, nothing was rising above the level of what Reisman called ground clutter.

"A lot of yelling. Not much else," he said.

CRISIS LIFE CYCLE
STEP SIX—DELIVER THE MESSAGE(S), MANAGE THE MEDIA MESSENGER (And they're only the messenger)

TRASK HEADQUARTERS
FOOT, NEW YORK
May 24, 2019 | 12:20 p.m.

"How many people work in that building?" The question came over the phone to Geeta Allen from Coke Stewart, a reporter with WJKA, the Washington, D.C. ABC affiliate station.

"The building is configured to house approximately 130 Trask employees. We can't say that's exactly how many people are in the building on any given day," Allen replied.

"So, is it safe to say 130 people are in the building?"

"No. It's safe to say the building can house 130 persons."

Nice to have the contingency Q&A handy, Allen thought. She was working from a set of prepared hypothetical questions and answers, Q&As, designed for use in the event of an inquiry regarding a crisis situation.

The WJKA reporter tried another track. "Geeta, do you know anyone who works in that building?"

THAT wasn't in the Q&A set. Allen was quiet for a moment. "I know a lot of people who work in Bethesda."

Stewart wasn't taking the "drop it" hint Allen just gave him. "But do you know anyone who works in that building?"

"Coke, I'm not going into a discussion of my personal life."

"That's not what I'm asking, Geeta."

"Let's agree to disagree. Is there anything else you need?"

Stewart was quiet.

"Coke, may I assume we're done?" Allen asked.

"No. Can you tell me the type of work that goes on in the building?"

"Mostly accounts receivable and payable." That was one of the prepared Q&A's she had at her disposal.

"Is that for the entire company?"

Allen paused. *Don't lie*, she thought, then replied, "Yes."

"Let me confirm. ALL of Trask's AR and AP takes place at the Udell Road site?"

"Yep."

"OK. Has that operation been interrupted at all?"

"The building is under a lockdown, and a gunman is running around inside."

"That's not what I mean, Geeta. Are you unable to conduct business as usual?"

"Since this incident started, I'd say you are correct."

Stewart was getting frustrated. "I mean is it hurting your long-term operations, Geeta? You know what I'm asking."

"Coke, like any technology operation, we have cloud back-ups, and we plan for redundancies in all of our IT work." That one was in the Q&A set.

"Are you using those redundancies?"

"Not yet, no." Chalk another answer up to the Q&As.

Stewart could see this was going nowhere, so he tried one more thing. "Geeta, has Trask recently fired any employees who work in the Udell Road building?"

That, too, was in the Q&A set. "I'm sorry, but we don't discuss employee situations."

"Does that mean you have recently fired someone?"

"It means we don't discuss employee situations. That's personal, and we keep it that way."

"But this could be germane to the story, Geeta."

"Coke, look," Allen was freelancing right now. "I know you have a job to do, and you have to ask questions that you may not get answers to. This is one of those situations. Please understand that there are some questions that I won't answer … no matter what the circumstances or how germane it may be to the story. Personal information about an employee [she almost said, "information about people we have fired"] is just off limits, no matter what the story."

"I understand, Geeta. Thank you."

"Thanks for your time, Coke."

She hung up and took a deep breath. She looked up to see John Taylor and Ed Reisman walking her way.

"Tough day at the P.R. shop?" Reisman said.

"No worse than others, I suppose. You here to make it easier or harder?"

Taylor sat down. "A bit of both."

"Our friend Ron Reynolds looked over the backgrounds of some board members and discovered a few things about them that we need to keep in our contingency Q&A back pocket," Reisman said, pushing a sheet of paper toward Allen.

"Personal delivery rather than an email? How very 1970s of you, Ed."

"We don't want a digital paper trail on this one, Geeta, so no email this time," Taylor said. The light mood she was trying to force into this meeting was gone. She looked at the paper and saw three names of Trask board members.

"Eric Trainor, lawyer, retired, and ... Jesus Christ ..."

"American Handgun Association board member, yeah," Reisman said.

"Read on," Taylor said.

"Augustine 'Gus' Henlopen, retired. AHA member since 1980." She shook her head. "It just gets better and better, doesn't it?"

"There's one more name," Reisman said. "Here's where it does get a little better."

Allen looked back at the paper, "Lorraine DellaBonvia, attorney, San Mateo, California. Chapter president of ... Parents Demand Action." She looked up at Reisman and Taylor. "I'm sorry, what's Parents Demand Action?"

"Possibly not as well-known as the AHA for sure, but it's a grassroots political action committee dedicated to passing what they call common sense gun laws," Taylor said. "They're big on issues that protect families. You sometimes hear of them more when there is a shooting at a school, but our situation is right up their alley."

"They're the antithesis to the AHA in this case, Geeta," Reisman said. "DellaBonvia is a chapter president in California. San Mateo is one of the organization's more active areas."

Things were still moving fast, and Allen needed a moment to wrap her head around the information she was just presented. "You don't want me to call Coke Stewart back to tell him this, do you?"

Reisman sat up a bit straighter, "No. Of course not. But let's just be aware of this information. Trask is a publicly traded company. If we can find out this level of information about our Board members . . ."

". . . so can the press," Allen said.

"This is material for our contingency Q&A set," Taylor said. "Ed and I are working on suggested verbiage, but we want your input on whatever we write."

Still taking this in, Allen thought, *So, if Stewart or someone asks me if any of our board members are AHA members, we can just say . . . what?*

"I have something drafted now," Reisman said. "We thought it best to be open. Say we don't closely track our board members outside interests . . ."

A quick study, Allen saw where the conversation was going. "We can say that and add that our board members are . . ."

". . . MAY BE," Taylor corrected her.

"Right, may be AHA members and some are also members of organizations like Parents Demand Action. I get it."

"Exactly," Taylor said. "I worked at a college that had a veterinary medicine program. It was frequently criticized for keeping animals on campus. The critters were there to help the school educate good veterinarians, but that didn't stop the critics from carping. When necessary, we would mention that many of the vet program students were members of PETA ... People for the Ethical Treatment of Animals."

"I get it. The same idea applies here. What our board members do on their own time is their own business. Their interests are varied, but regardless we don't speak for them."

"I'd turn that around for a press response, Geeta. Say we don't speak for them first, then follow with what they do on their own time yadda-yadda," Reisman said. "And emphasize that our board members have an array of outside interests. None of them apply to Trask International. I'll send you and John a draft of what I wrote for contingency Q&As. It isn't perfect, so I would appreciate your help on this."

Allen nodded. "Anything else coming to me via non-email paper trail?"

Reisman just looked down. "Maybe."

OK, so Trask International supports Parents Demand Action and a gun lobby or two, not to mention we have two board members active in the AHA and one active in the antithesis of the AHA. And all we have to do is achieve a Yin/Yang we can live with, Allen thought.

Taylor shrugged. "Darkest before the dawn, Geeta."

Allen looked at Taylor and thought of her friend, Joe Barron. "We're not in that building right now, John."

CRISIS LIFE CYCLE
STEP SEVEN—MONITOR AND CORRECT

INSIDE THE BUILDING
May 24, 2019 | 12:07 p.m.
It starts to get very real

The Glock was easy enough for Tomlinson to load. Just press the magazine release with his right thumb, letting the empty sixteen-round magazine drop to the floor. Next, he pushed the slide forward as he inserted a new magazine, letting the slide snap back into position. He was ready to keep firing.

The sixteen rounds Tomlinson just used up were randomly fired throughout the building. Nothing toward the windows leading out the building. After what seemed like only a minute passed, the Glock's magazine was empty again, so he pulled a fresh magazine from his pocket, and quickly pushed the slide on the weapon to be sure nothing was in the firing chamber as he slid a new sixteen-round magazine into the weapon. He again pushed the slide to put a round in the chamber.

That's when he screwed up. He didn't let the weapon's slide snap back on its own. He manually pushed the slide, and the weapon immediately jammed.

"Glock 101, dumbass," Tomlinson muttered as he attempted to fix his weapon.

Tom Larry saw this. He was about to run into an office when Tomlinson jammed the Glock. Larry was a twenty-year Trask man and a gun owner. He knew a jammed weapon when he saw one.

He also saw an opening to end this insanity.

He lunged at Tomlinson, grabbing the shooter's right arm.

Tomlinson was struggling with the Glock when Larry grabbed him.

It wasn't a fair fight.

Tomlinson was 44, 6'3," and about 240 pounds. He wasn't muscular, but he was in good enough shape.

Larry was 55, 5'8" and about 150 pounds. He pulled down hard on Tomlinson's right arm, pushing his weight against Tomlinson, throwing him off balance long enough to fall to the floor.

Larry fell to the ground with Tomlinson. This physical struggle was definitely not action movie caliber.

Had Larry landed on Tomlinson, he might have been able to pin him. But he fell to the floor on his opponent's left.

Tomlinson brought his left arm up, pulling his left forearm across his face. In one fast motion he snapped his elbow to the left toward Larry, hitting him square in his right eye socket. The force snapped Larry's head back, and he did a barrel roll to his left. He was far enough away from Tomlinson to start getting back on his feet.

I'm in trouble. Get out of here, Larry thought.

He and Tomlinson came to their feet at the same time.

His gun is still jammed. I can get away, Larry thought.

He was wrong. He couldn't get away. Larry hadn't seen the shotgun slung over Tomlinson's right shoulder.

Pulling the shotgun over this shoulder, Tomlinson pointed it at Larry and fired. A single 2 ¾ inch slug slammed into the upper right side of Larry's chest. He fell to the floor like a ragdoll.

That burns, Larry thought.

It was the force of the round's impact that put Larry on the floor. He looked down and saw the wound, started to feel a surging tightness in his chest. The discomfort from tightness was quickly overtaken by an intense burning sensation that started at the wound and passed through his body in seconds.

The amount of blood coming out of him might have terrified Larry to the point of further panic. But he was starting to black out.

I'm dying. It was his last thought.

Tomlinson ran down the hallway about 40 or 50 feet and around a corner from where he and Larry fought, pulling the ski mask off of his head. His Glock was still jammed. He saw an open doorway and ducked inside.

Behind a desk about 15 feet away from Larry, Suzy Torres watched the horror of her coworker's death. The blast from Tomlinson's shotgun forced her to look away at first. When she looked back, she saw Larry's blood-soaked body lying motionless on the floor.

If the gunshots weren't enough to scare people in the building, then Torres' screams were.

"DO WE NEED THIS STUFF?"
15 MILES AWAY - ARACAE MOTORS - GAITHERSBURG, MARYLAND
May 24, 2019 | 12:30 p.m.

John Miller was a retired U.S. Postal Service employee. His wife, Dorothy, worked in the Trask building in Bethesda. Dorothy was 60, and John was 70. Like many retirees, he wanted to work to keep himself occupied, so he had taken a job at a local auto dealership, Aracae Motors. It was relatively easy work selling cars; since he didn't need to make money to make ends meet, he could just enjoy the casual interactions with people that happened each day and appreciate the occasional commission check.

His presence satisfied both his management, who always wanted closers on the sales team, and the casual customer who just wanted someone at the dealership they could talk to. Frank Aracae, the dealership owner, described John as "a whitehead," a senior citizen. He'd say "Customers like buying cars from a whitehead."

Miller wasn't bad at selling. Just two days earlier he sold a three-year-old Lincoln SUV to a man who said he had lots of business to take care of with the car. *Not really a strange answer,* John thought, but it was odd that he made a point of being vague about what he'd do with the car. At the end of the day, though, a customer's use of any vehicle they buy is none of his business.

On this particular day he was relaxing at his desk reading the newspaper. His younger coworkers teased him for reading an actual newspaper and not using Twitter or some other digital app to get the news.

Paper is reliable and standby, he thought. *What is it the kids say? It's a legacy app, and I'm sticking with it.*

It wasn't exactly kids who said that about newspapers, but anyone younger than Miller was, from his perspective, a kid.

About 30 feet from where Miller was seated were several large-screen televisions hanging from the ceiling in the customer service waiting area. Each was tuned to different local TV stations. John was accustomed to hearing a cacophony of noise coming from three different TV sets. He thought he was pretty good at differentiating between what each TV was broadcasting. *The Price is Right* on the far left, *Love it or List It* reruns in the middle, and ESPN's *SportsCenter* on the far right.

At that moment, though, John realized all three TV sets were showing the same thing. The left set was still set to the local CBS affiliate. The other two sets had been set to local ABC and NBC affiliates. The local news operations had kicked in, interrupting programming, showing something live.

"... over one-hundred people are trapped ..."" ... unidentified gunman inside ..."

"... Police are very concerned about fatalities ..."

What the hell?

"The Trask offices off of Independence Boulevard are in a real-life hostage situation ..."

"... reports coming in of multiple gunshot wounds. But no one as yet has been able to enter the building."

What the hell? Dorothy works there!!!

John moved quickly—as quickly as a 70-year-old with a carbon fiber knee can move—to get closer to the televisions and listen in. He focused on the ABC affiliate, WJKA.

"This is Coke Stewart, and I am outside of the Trask building at 1041 Udell Road in Bethesda. At approximately 11:30 a.m. today at least one heavily armed man drove an SUV through the front door of the Trask building off Independence Boulevard, exited the vehicle, and began shooting at anyone and anything..."

Dorothy? Where is Dorothy?

John pulled his phone from his pocket and was about to call his wife when another call came in. It was an unfamiliar number, but he did recognize the exchange. The call was coming from inside the Trask building. He tapped answer.

"John?"

"Dorothy? I saw on TV... What's going on?"

"John, I'm ok." She could easily recognize the fear in her husband's voice. "A bunch of us are in a conference room. We don't know where the guy with the gun is, so we're taking turns calling family and being really quiet. We might be too loud otherwise, so I have to let someone else call their family."

"Dorothy, you have to get out of there!"

"I can't, John. Not yet. We're trying to reach the police to see what's happening. We have heard sirens."

"Dorothy, please..."

"I love you, John."

"I love you, too, Dorothy."

"I'll call again as soon as I can."

John stared at his phone for a minute. Again, the news anchor's voice caught his attention.

"There you see the vehicle we think was used to drive through the doorway at Trask International. We cannot ascertain from this angle what condition the vehicle is in, but the rear seems to be intact, and it is not, as far as we can see, on fire."

John looked closely at the image on the television as the camera zoomed in.

"People are probably recording the license tag as we zoom in on the vehicle," the reporter said as the camera quickly zoomed to a close up of the rear of the SUV. The anchor continued talking, pulling out words to fill the air. TV news hates dead air.

John didn't need to see the license tag. His line of vision went first to the brand—a Lincoln SUV, then he focused on the decal on the left rear of the vehicle. The decal identified the dealership where the SUV was purchased. ARACAE MOTORS!

Holy shit. That's the car I sold!!!

CRISIS LIFE CYCLE
STEP EIGHT—UPDATE AND FOLLOW UP

THE CACOPHONY GETS EVEN LOUDER
CONFERENCE ROOM - TRASK HEADQUARTERS
May 24, 2019 | 12:31 p.m.

Geeta Allen, Taylor, and Reisman watched Coke Stewart's report on television.

"He seemed to hit all the marks," Allen said.

Then a mark was missed.

"Trask International uses the building for accounts payable and receivable records. Although a spokesperson for the company said they are not using their backup systems, the building and the operations it houses are definitely compromised. This is Coke Stewart reporting."

"What the . . ." Allen was flabbergasted. "I never said that."

"I know you didn't, Geeta. I was less than 20 feet away when you spoke to him on the phone," Taylor said.

"We need to correct him AND let our customers know we aren't crippled," Allen said. She turned to her laptop to start composing a tweet.

> @TraskIntl
> **Just to correct @WJKANews incorrectly stated our work is compromised. That isn't true. We have backups and work is progressing as it should.**

The above message was retweeted by Trask International's customer service team.

Next, to make sure she made nice with the press, Allen tweeted the following:

> **@TraskIntl**
> No hard feelings @WJKANews. We're only human. Every-
> body makes mistakes.

"Stevens probably won't like that," Taylor said.

Like I give a fuck, Allen thought, then said, "Goes with the job, I suppose."

"Nicely done, Geeta. I know what a pain in the ass dealing with the press in this situation can be."

Reisman had his own minor snafu to clear up, putting a call in to Sylvester Moore.

"What's up, Ed?"

"Sly, please refrain from language like saying 'yay' in your customer service tweets. At least for now?"

"Why? We want to be responsive and friendly. Letting customers know the service bots are disabled is, for most customers, a cause for celebration."

"Sly, it's the REASON you disabled the bots that is no cause for celebration. Look, we cannot seem even remotely glib about this situation. Everything we say is going under a microscope, so please be careful."

"Understood, Ed. Thanks."

> **@MontCoPolice**
> Attention #NewsMedia. Please do not fly your helicopters
> directly over the Trask International building.

Two minutes later.

> Attention #NewsMedia, thank you for pulling back on
> your helicopter flights. A time and place for a news brief-
> ing will be announced shortly.

CRISIS LIFE CYCLE
STEP ONE (AGAIN)—IDENTIFY AND NOTIFY

ARACAE MOTORS
GAITHERSBURG, MARYLAND
May 24, 2019 | 12:32 p.m.

Miller needed to tell someone what he just discovered. A car with an Aracae Motors sticker on it played a role in a mass shooting. A car he may well have just recently sold to someone. Someone who may be responsible for the insanity happening in Bethesda.

Miller looked around for his immediate supervisor when he overheard the receptionist calling Frank Aracae, the dealership owner, and saying, "Mr. Aracae, there is a Coke Stewart on the line. He's with the local TV news, and he'd like to speak to you."

So much for telling someone about it, Miller said to himself.

He started pacing just to keep his mind occupied and not think about Dorothy.

He was nervous, but he knew the situation inside the Trask building was far worse than any anxiety he was feeling.

EYES ON THE CRISIS
May 24, 2019 | 12:18 p.m.

Sergeant Bill LaTulipe and Officer Tom Drew were the first police on site at Udell Road.

The days are over where a police department would wait for a S.W.A.T. team to assemble before entering a building where an active shooter is located. Lives could be lost in the time it takes for the team to arrive and decide on a tactical formation before entering the building. The mass shooting at Columbine High

School in Colorado twenty years earlier, where two armed individuals murdered fifteen students, teachers, and administrators, taught police departments and the communities they served throughout the country a painful lesson: waiting until you are ready to enter an active shooter site is a recipe for more murder and mayhem.

Instead, Sergeant LaTulipe had a tremendous amount of decision-making authority. He and Drew would be the first to go inside as more backup, including the S.W.A.T. team, was on the way.

Tomlinson heard the sirens of LaTulipe's and Drew's cars; counting two vehicles, he kept moving and kept shooting until his Glock jammed, and he encountered and killed Larry.

Entering the building past the SUV, LaTulipe and Officer Drew quickly scanned the situation. A heavily damaged Lincoln SUV was striding atop what was left of a reception desk. The front of the SUV was missing its grill, headlights shattered, hood bent in. It appeared to be the classic way the front of a car collapses in order to protect the occupant.

Sure enough, the interior of the passenger compartment had only minor damage. The driver's side door was open, and LaTulipe could see the air bag had deployed. The desk where Carl Wilson sat was shattered. Wilson's lifeless body was beneath what was left of the desk. The light gray carpeting in the lobby turned black from the blood from Wilson's chest wound. About 45 feet away, a woman was lying face down; the back of her skull was missing.

"Carnage," was all LaTulipe said aloud.

"It's probably gonna be a whole lot worse," Drew said. They heard screams on the second floor and quickly moved up the stairs.

The second floor was filled with long hallways interrupted by cubicle farms and the occasional office or conference room. Offices had no windows. Most of the conference rooms did. When

JOE DIORIO | 89

he reached the top of the stars, LaTulipe turned right to slowly move down the hallway. One body was on the floor. He had bled out before anyone could get to him. The police later identified this victim as Tom Larry.

Remembering his military training to "keep your head on a swivel," LaTulipe looked back at Drew, who acknowledged he saw the body. It was time to keep silent as they moved through the building. That was the moment LaTulipe realized that, while he and Drew were being quiet, the building itself had suddenly become very quiet. The two officers could hear gunshots as they approached the building, but not now. And no one was calling out for help.

"Oh, thank god!" came a raspy voice seemingly out of nowhere. Someone, a woman, was crouched behind a desk, not far from Larry's body. LaTulipe put up his hand to silence her. He looked around as he moved closer.

"Are you alone?" he whispered. "Just nod or shake your head."

She nodded.

"Are you hurt?"

She shook her head. She was wearing her ID badge on a lanyard. Her name was Suzy Torres.

LaTulipe looked back at Drew and mouthed the words, "Help her out."

Drew and LaTulipe helped Torres to her feet, and Drew led her out of the building. LaTulipe crouched down behind the desk where Torres was hiding, pulled out his cell phone and texted his commander. He used one of the messages in his Notes app: a message the social media committee had devised a few months back. The objective was to have most of a message written in advance and just text the message without having to create something from scratch. This message needed some tweaking, but it was easier than having to rewrite the whole thing. And with a gunman on the loose, it was a damn sight more secure than talking on a radio. With no idea where the shooter was, he didn't want the bad guy or bad guys to hear him.

His text message to Captain Kelly Mayer, the commanding officer in charge of the site, read:

> "AM IN THE BUILDING. ALL QUIET. AT LEAST THREE DEAD. SHOOTER LOCATION NOT KNOWN."

He made sure his cell was in silent mode before sending the message.

Mayer's response came back quickly.

> "COPY. CONTINUE LOOKING FOR EMPLOYEES. SWAT IS EN ROUTE."

LaTulipe placed his phone back in the belt holster. Staying low, he moved slowly down the hallway, leading himself by gunpoint. He came upon another open "team center" and noticed three people hiding behind desks. One of them was Ted Lewiston, who couldn't stop shaking. Again, he motioned to be still, approached them.

"Show me your hands, please," he said in a stage whisper. All three held up their hands.

"Are you hurt?" All three shook their heads.

"OK, get up if you can, and follow me. Please stay close."

Lewiston stayed down. LaTulipe bent over him. "Sir, can you move?"

"Yes," Lewiston's voice was faint.

"You're safe," LaTulipe said. "Just follow me and your co-workers."

He led them to the stairwell, down the stairs, and to the north doorway. It was a few more steps to take, but he wouldn't have to ask anyone to climb over a dead body and a crushed car.

Arriving at the north entrance, he could see Montgomery County police in the parking lot. He radioed the site commander to let them know that three people were exiting the building, that they were not armed, and they were not injured.

This process would become easier once the S.W.A.T. teams arrived.

The work by the police would continue on site and at headquarters.

MONTGOMERY COUNTY POLICE HEADQUARTERS
May 24, 2019 | 12:25 p.m.

After the two cops entered the building, calls from the public and press continued coming into the police department in droves. Public Information Officer Sergeant Brenda Conner was fielding the calls.

"Yes, there is a report of an active shooter at an office building in Bethesda."

"No, we cannot confirm yet if it is the Trask Building."

"No, we do not know if there are injuries."

"As far as we know, it is an active situation."

"We ask that you stand by for more information."

"I suggest you follow our Twitter account for more details."

"Yes, please follow our Twitter."

"Twitter. Please follow our Twitter."

How many times do I have to say check Twitter?

As she spoke, Sergeant Conner opened Twitter on her department laptop, then opened a folder called, "EmergencySitTweets." These were a series of Twitter messages that the department developed during quiet times, "blue sky days" is the term they used, that were approved for use during a crisis. And a report of an active shooter is definitely a crisis.

The story continued to unfold on social media. One of the first updates was from the local police department, sent out by Sergeant Conner:

> **@MontCoPolice**
> **We are on scene at a shooting at the Trask building at 1041 Udell Road, Bethesda. We are doing a methodical search and working closely with other first responder organizations @MontcoFD @MontcoEMT. We will soon announce a staging location where more information can be distributed.**
> 12:27 p.m. - May 24, 2019

Her messages continued. There is a predetermined pattern of messages that the police department decided to send out. This planning was done during one of those "blue sky days," as crisis planners like to call them, when planning can be done logically, with thought put into the messages. Sending out random messages in the heat of the moment can lead to confusion. Not that other people using social media didn't feed into the confusion. First responders need to be clear and brief.

The tweets from individuals, adding to the cacophony, continued unabated by time, a lack of facts, and driven by emotion.

> **@ThisIsLen**
> **Why aren't the police saying anything?**

> **@Melissa**
> **Is traffic snarled near the mall?**

> **@MDA**
> **Here is a link with addresses to GOP congressmen who oppose gun legislation.**

@TwoBirs
Where is this happening?

@Shopaholic
OMG, are they shooting the mall?

@SanityinMedia
No, idiot, not the mall. An office building nearby. Your
stores are safe.

@DanBDere
Hey, watch your language asshole

@LokiKnows
Look whoze talking

@ForSanity
Wouldn't happen with better gun laws

@AHAMan
No it'd be worse with more gun laws, OK?

@SanityinMedia
Can we puleeze not talk about gun laws right now?

@ForSanity
Sure, when do you want to talk about them

@HagarTheMan
Read this (attaches a link to a 12-page manifesto from
a gun control lobby)

@AHAMan
No, ace, read THIS! (attaches link to a 20-page gun owner freedom statement)

And on and on went the conversation. Some had hashtags: #TraskShooter #TraskandAHA #AHASucks #AHA4Evah which led to even more chatter about the subject of the Bethesda shooting and into gun rights in general.

Social media professionals like Conner and Allen understand they are talking amid a shouting match. The challenge is to make your social posts stand out. For Trask International and the Montgomery County Police Department, that work started years ago, long before the name Mel Tomlinson came into play.

The police department and Trask International followed standard nomenclature for twitter handles, recognizable artwork to accompany the tweet, and the frequency and type of tweets they released. Trask advertised the availability of its social media presence in all marketing material. Occasionally, Trask would post a live video via a social media outlet. The objective is twofold: get more eyeballs looking at you AND build a level of familiarity. Both enterprises understand that you have to own the story, whatever the story is, or it will own you.

By keeping their messages clear, short, and direct. By maintaining a consistent presence on social media. And by not engaging with tweets that are little more than distractions, Trask and the police were able to remain above the digital shouting match that is Twitter. The shouting continued, of course, but it was having little effect on the messages the police wanted to get out to the public.

INSIDE THE BUILDING
May 24, 2019 | 12:35 p.m.

LaTulipe briefed his commander via text regarding his location in the building as a command post was being established in the main parking lot of the building. Now the police had to figure out WHERE in the building the shooter was hiding. And how they were going to get him out and rescue the scores of people still inside.

When Captain Mayer arrived, LaTulipe and Drew's cars were haphazardly parked outside of the building. Mayer deployed five officers, who arrived when she did, to set up a perimeter around the building. Standard orders: no one comes in or goes out without her knowing about it. The S.W.A.T. command team arrived minutes later.

Mayer signaled to the three S.W.A.T. teams to move in and start going through the building, one for each floor of the building. All teams were to find anyone who was inside and provide first aid to those who needed it. Anyone who could move on their own would be instructed to get out of the building. Fast. Four additional officers, each armed with a shotgun, stood guard at the stairwell at the opposite end of the building from where the SUV entered. Employees would be directed to exit there.

One of the teams was instructed to rendezvous with LaTulipe. Mayer had sent him a text to hold position until they arrived.

She corralled Officer Drew right after he dropped Suzy Torrez off with the EMTs.

"What can you tell me, Officer Drew?" Mayer asked. She was no nonsense and straightforward when it came to a heavy situation like this.

"Bullet holes throughout the first and second floors, Captain," Drew said. "Three dead. Two on the first floor and one on the second. May be more, but the shooting stopped seconds after Bill and I entered the building. I suspect the gunman is hiding."

Mayer's mind was racing. *Hiding? Great. How do I distinguish a door that has a killer behind it and one with innocent people hiding?* Then her thoughts moved on to another subject. *One hundred thirty people. One shooter. Where to start looking?*

A canceled hair salon appointment provided the location of the gunman.

SILVER SPRING, MARYLAND
MAY 24, 2019 | 12:20 P.M.

Tara Glassover was one of four reporters for WDCN, the all-news radio station in Washington, D.C. One for each of three shifts throughout the day. This Friday she was going to get her hair trimmed at the salon, but she had worked an extra shift the day before—cutbacks reduced the staff at the radio station, but the need to provide news 24/7 didn't go away. It made no sense, but what does in the news business?

She had a 1 p.m. appointment at her hairdresser, but she decided to skip it. *Too tired*, she thought. *I'll just chill at home.*

Great plan. Until her phone rang.

It was the news director, Marc Tilling. "Tara, something is going on over at the Trask building in Bethesda. I need someone to go and check it out."

"Something is going on?"

"Yes."

"Like . . . what?" She wasn't driving to Bethesda for a false fire alarm or some other softball story. Even after rush hour, traffic on the Washington/Baltimore Beltway was a bitch. Glassover knew (1) she was being borderline insubordinate, (2) she wasn't 100 percent secure in her job, but (3) she knew there would be short-term pain at the radio station if one more news reporter abruptly left via firing or resignation. So, she wasn't getting up off her ass for a "disturbance" in an office building that's near the Bethesda shopping mall.

Mall plus beltway traffic? No thank you.

"You're not looking at Twitter?"

"Only if I absolutely have to. You know I hate social media." A strange comment coming from someone working in an industry that desperately needs social media for readers, listeners, viewers, and relevance.

"Sorry, Tara. Buzz on the police radio and on Twitter says there is an active shooter situation in Bethesda. People are trapped inside the Trask International building on Udell Road."

Glassover paused. She knew people who worked in the building. She didn't say that to Tilling, only uttering an agreement to drive to the site and see what she can learn.

As soon as Tilling was off the phone, and she was in her SUV, she flipped through her contacts. "Richard Davie, programmer, Trask." She tapped the call button. Davie answered.

"Richard, it's Tara Glassover. We met a while back at a Kennedy Center event."

"I remember, Tara. Right now, it is kind of a bad time."

"I heard. Are you OK?"

"Yes, but I can't talk. Listen, call me back at this number." He gave her another number. She could tell by the exchange it was another phone in the Trask building.

She was driving as she was talking and couldn't write down the number. She instead tried committing it to memory. She punched the new number in—at least she thought it was the new number. It wasn't, and a different voice answered.

"Hello."

"Hi, is Richard Davie there? It's Tara Glassover."

"Sorry. It's only me in here."

"Are you in the Trask International building?"

The voice laughed. "Yeah, I'm there."

"Are you in an office?"

"A conference room, I think."

Strange. Why wouldn't someone who works there—why the hell else would someone be in that dank, depressing office building—know the difference between a conference room and an office?

She decided to keep the conversation going. "So, do you work there?"

"I used to."

"Used to?"

"Yeah."

Was he visiting someone? "Why are you there now?"

"I'm the guy. I'm the one they want."

It took a second or two to process that answer.

"I'm the guy shooting the place up." It was Tomlinson speaking, Glassover would soon learn. Tomlinson had heard Dorothy Miller's description of him, and he instinctively used the same words she did.

Glassover managed to get some words out. "Who . . . who are you?"

"I'm Mel."

"Mel . . . what?" This was a stretch to get his name, but she figured she'd try.

"Mel Tomlinson."

"OK, Mel Tomlinson." She said his name to make sure she had it right. People will sometimes correct you if you pronounce their name incorrectly. Tomlinson didn't, so she figured her pronunciation was on the money. *That's important for when I go live with this.*

"I'm Tara Glassover from WDCN, Mel. Do you want to keep talking?"

"Sure. I've heard you on the radio."

Watch the damn traffic, Tara! A Toyota Prius almost ran into her when she was changing lanes. "Thanks. So where in the building are you?"

"Second floor."

Let's try another home run swing. "Did you shoot people?"

"I shot my guns, yeah. I guess I got a few. Right now, my gun is jammed so I decided to hide in here."

This is definitely better than talking to a hairdresser.

"Are the police nearby?"

"I'm not sure. Everything is pretty quiet inside. Lots of police sirens outside."

"I know. I'm driving there right now."

"I probably should turn myself in, shouldn't I?"

"That's probably a good idea, Mel." Tara was amazed she could keep talking. *This is one helluva story!*

Yes, that thought—*helluva story*—crosses the mind of every news reporter every now and then. Everyone who works in journalism knows they won't always get the hottest story. And they acknowledge that all stories have value. Job number one for any news reporter is to report the news, regardless of whether it's dull or exciting. But there is a big difference in the type of news you are reporting. The school board approving a budget is an important story because it can affect a lot of people. But coming face-to-face—OK, phone-to-phone—with a potential mass murderer is way different. And way better. Glassover hated to admit it, but the adage is true; if it bleeds, it leads, and she's on the phone with the guy causing the bleeding.

Don't go live with it, Glassover. Not yet. You don't know this guy's state of mind. He's talking to you. He knows you are a reporter.

"Is it OK if we keep talking on the record, Mel?" she asked.

"Sure."

That was all she needed. *Everything he's said so far is fair game.* She can get to Bethesda and tell the police she's been talking to the shooter—OK, alleged shooter—and still have what has transpired in their conversation for a story.

Since she was playing a hot hand, she tried again.

"Do you want to surrender, Mel?"

"Yeah . . . but how about I surrender to you?"

She paused to again get the dryness out of her throat. "Me?"

"Yeah."

"I'm gonna need to let the police know about that, Mel."

"OK, that's fine."

She reconfirmed Mel was on the second floor of the building. "Mel, are there any windows where you are?"

"Yeah."

"Can you see out of the windows? Can you see other buildings?" What buildings he saw would tell her where in the building he was hiding.

"I can see that MarLock Aerospace building out beyond the parking lot."

OK, he's on the west side of the building on the upper floor.

"OK, Mel. Promise me you'll stay put."

Glassover did not expect a chipper reception from the Montgomery County police. They were notoriously insular, rarely talking to the press unless it was absolutely necessary. At least that was the perception by the press. She turned right onto Udell Road and immediately saw the police barricade. A MontCo police officer was waving her off. She put the small "PRESS" placard on the dashboard of her SUV, parked, and got out.

"You can't stay there," one of the officers at the blockade shouted.

"Where is your commanding officer? I'm Tara Glassover with WDCN and I need to talk to him."

"A lot of people need to talk to my C.O., Tara Glassover with WDCN. Now MOVE YOUR CAR!"

She knew this conversation wouldn't be easy. She had to play her trump card right then and there.

"The shooter's name is Mel Tomlinson, and he wants to surrender to me."

The officer waving her off stopped waving and stared at her. "What?"

"I know who the shooter is, and I know where in the building he's hiding. He said he wants to surrender to me."

"How the hell do you know that? And why the hell should I believe you?" He took a few steps toward her.

She held up her phone. "We talked." She took one step back toward her car. If the cop decided he wanted to confiscate her phone, she was going to get in the SUV and hightail it out of there.

OK, blockade cop isn't budging. Time to try playing my last hand. "Look, you don't have to put me in touch with anyone. I have enough material for a story, and I can just go with what I have, OK? In fact, why don't I just leave and file my story right now?" She turned to get in her SUV.

The cop stopped walking toward her. "Wait, don't go. Just wait here. Stay put, OK?" He used his radio to call someone. He repeated himself before making a call on his radio, "Just stay put, OK?"

He just told me to stay put. That is becoming a common request, Tara thought. She stationed herself by the door to her SUV and waited.

Momentarily, a Montgomery County Police SUV pulled up next to the cop Glassover was talking to. Captain Kelly Mayer emerged. She wasted little time, talking as soon as she looked at Glassover.

"You the one who's friends with the shooter?" she said.

"He's not my friend. I don't even know him. But I have talked to him," Glassover replied. *This jerk isn't going to bully me.*

"So, what's up with your friend?"

"You have a listening problem, commander? He isn't my friend. I'm with the press, and I accidentally talked to him on the phone."

"OK, let's start over. Show me your ID."

Glassover produced her press card. "Now you show me your ID." She has worked with local police before and did not take any B.S. from anyone.

Mayer took her press card and looked at the reporter over her glasses. "I don't have time for attitude, young lady."

"Me, neither. And you can call me Tara, Ms. Glassover, or just Glassover." She wasn't letting anyone get away with the "young lady" barb.

Mayer pointed at her badge. "Here's my ID, OK? Look, this is a bad situation, and I don't have time for games."

"Then don't play them."

Mayer let Glassover's snide remark pass, instead pressing her questions for the young reporter. "How did you happen to talk to the shooter?"

Glassover filled her in, explaining where he apparently was in the building.

"You say he's on the second floor on the west side?"

"Yeah, he said he can see the MarLock Aerospace building out of a window of the room he's in."

"OK, first, MarLock Aerospace is on the *east* side of the building."

That slowed Glassover's roll. "OK, sorry. This is coming at me fast."

"It's coming at all of us fast. But thank you. This is really helpful."

"He said he wants to surrender to me."

Mayer was looking down at her radio, listening to a report from the S.W.A.T. team. "Not happening. How did you manage to talk to him again?"

"I basically called the wrong number," she again held up her phone.

"May I see that number?"

Glassover hesitated. Mayer spoke.

"I'm not icing you out here. He talked to you. He said he wants to surrender to you, so I think it makes sense for you to talk to him again. But somewhere in the conversation you will have to hand things off to someone skilled with hostage negotiations."

"Hostages? He said he was alone."

Mayer motioned toward the Trask building. "Right now, there are possibly over 130 people in there, Tara, including the shooter. Nobody is coming out on their own, and I have to figure out a way to help them get out safely."

One hundred thirty people? Glassover knew the situation was bad, but JESUS.

Keep your composure. Act like you already know. "So, what's the guy want?"

"We're still figuring that out. Right now, we need to disarm and arrest him, and get the people inside to safety. Now, may I please see your phone, so I can get the number you called? That will go a long way toward helping us know for sure where he is."

One more moment of hesitancy passed before Mayer spoke again.

"Look, Tara. We need each other here. The police try to keep people safe, and every day I work with the press to get important safety information out to people. I'm not trying to play a game here. You made an important first step. He's talked to you, and by what you tell me he's comfortable doing that. Let's do this together."

Glassover pulled up the number and handed her phone to Captain Mayer, who wrote down the number and handed the phone back.

"OK, Tara, thanks. Let's go do some good."

The phone number Glassover called was connected to a landline in the building. Unfortunately, the one person who understood the maze-like patchwork of telephone exchanges in the building, especially what office held what number, wasn't available. He or she was either still in the building or had escaped and was nowhere to be found. The phone number, then, was good for talking to Tomlinson, but not for locating him. That would require some person-to-person negotiations.

Soon Glassover, Mayer, and Officer Caleb Brown, a Montgomery County Police hostage negotiator, were ready. Glassover set her phone on speaker mode and called the number. The phone only rang once.

"Hello."

"Hi, Mel, it's Tara Glassover again."

"Hey."

"Listen, I'm outside of the building right now."

"OK."

"Do you still want to surrender to me?"

Long pause.

"Anyone with you?"

Glassover looked at Mayer and Brown, who nodded.

"Yes, Mel, I'm here with Captain Mayer and Officer Caleb Brown. He'd like to talk to you if that's OK."

Another pause.

"You stay on the line, OK?"

Mayer and Brown nodded.

"Hi, Mel, my name is Caleb. OK if I call you Mel?"

"Sure."

"Mel, there are a lot of people in that building right now. A lot of them are pretty scared. We sure would like to get them out without any problem."

"I'm just sitting here."

"That's good." *Offer encouragement*, Brown thought before continuing. "Mel, Tara tells me you can see the MarLock Aerospace building out of your window. Is that true?"

"Yeah, why?"

"No reason. I just have a cousin who works there." Brown lied about the cousin, but he did just confirm Tomlinson's whereabouts in the building. At least the hallway he is in. *Now, keep talking*, Brown thought. "You know anyone who works at MarLock Aerospace?"

"No."

As Brown talked Mayer stepped a few feet away and made a call to Frank Reardon, the retired Montgomery County detective. She needed to know how many conference rooms are on the second floor, east side of the building.

"Frank, it's Kelly Mayer."

"Hey, Cap. What's the situation?"

"Frank, we think we know where the shooter is in the building. I need to know how many conference rooms there are on the exterior wall of the building's east side, second floor. You know Trask executives, right?"

"Understood, Kelly. Standby." Mayer didn't need to explain.

Reardon set up a three-way call with Ed Reisman to relay the question. Reisman brought Burt Schorr into the conversation. He was still on Highway 50.

"There are two conference rooms in that upper hallway. One is connected to an executive office," Schorr told Reisman.

Mayer relayed that information to Caleb Brown, who had some conversational sleight of hand he wanted to try; a tactic to narrow down Tomlinson's location in the building.

"Mel, my cousin who works over at MarLock Aerospace is an executive. He has a really cool office that's connected to a conference room. Is that like the room you're in?"

Mel was quiet.

"It's OK, Mel. I'm just reminiscing about my cousin's office. It's pretty cool."

"There's no office connected to this room."

OK, NOW we know where he is.

"I want to surrender to Tara Glassover," Tomlinson said.

"I'd like to do that, Mel," Brown said. "But I need to be absolutely sure it is a safe situation. And the only way I can do that is if I am 100 percent certain you are unarmed. That means you have to come out of the room you are in, unarmed, show that your hands are empty, and let one of our officers escort you out of the building."

No response.

Brown thought quickly. "Tell you what. Just walk with officers to the building exit and Tara will be right outside of the building. You can speak to her there." Brown was careful not to say "surrender to police officers," or anyone else. Glassover felt her stomach drop when she heard that. Brown kept talking.

"I need to think about this," Tomlinson said.

"That's fine, Mel," Brown responded. "Can I call you back in, say, five minutes?"

"Sure."

"OK, I'm gonna call you from a different number because the battery on Tara's phone is getting low."

Glassover was about to say something about her phone being fully charged when Mayer squeezed her arm and gave her a "not now" look. Brown relayed a different number to Tomlinson, who agreed to the change in phones.

"We need this on a secure line, Tara," Mayer said.

"One that you're recording?" Glassover asked.

"Something like that, yes," Mayer said. She didn't look up at Glassover. She was thinking about the situation at hand.

Mayer's mind was racing. *One hundred and thirty people in there. One shooter*, she thought. Even with some degree of confidence of the shooter's location, getting everyone out safely was going to be tough.

"Switchboard at HQ is overheating," Mayer heard one of her officers say. Most of the calls were from family of employees, but a huge number of calls were coming from inside the building. Trapped Traskers wanted to know what was going on and how they could safely get out. *Worse yet*, she thought, *some of the Trask employees may try to exit the building on their own. Who is who? And will Tomlinson start picking people off if they do try to leave the building?* People needed police escorts out of there.

"How much do we say on social media, Captain?" Caleb Brown asked rhetorically. "Shooter may have his own phone and can see what we're telling people through Twitter."

"I'm aware of that, Officer Brown," Mayer said. She hated when anyone started mansplaining anything to her, especially when it came from a subordinate. But while Mayer quietly seethed at Brown's condescending tone, she heard Glassover muttering an obscenity.

"My fucking boss."

Mayer smiled. *Time to keep everyone positive*, she thought, then turned to Glassover. "You kiss your mother with that mouth?"

Glassover was looking at her phone as she cursed. She didn't look up. "Sorry, we use Slack for internal communications, and my boss is obsessed with it."

"Slack?"

"It's a comms tool for communication among groups. Basically, it's an internal messaging system that's only used by a group of people. It's supposed to make communication among a team easier . . . *except* when one person using it has diarrhea of the keyboard."

Mayer thought about what she just heard. "The group conversations on Slack . . . are they private?"

"Yes," Glassover said, still not looking up. "Doesn't make them any less annoying."

"Let me be sure I get that, Tara. No one outside of a defined group can see messages in Slack."

"Correct."

Mayer thought aloud, "Wonder if Trask uses Slack."

"They do," Glassover said. "My contact—the guy I was trying to call when I ended up talking to Tomlinson—has a Slack account. He said it was implemented company-wide by Trask I.T. Everyone has it on their phones."

Mayer quickly turned to Officer Brown. "Find a Trask employee who can help us use Slack." Then to Glassover she said, "I need a crash course on using Slack, stat!"

"You're gonna hate it," Glassover said.

"I don't have to like it if it helps me save some lives."

Within seconds Officer Brown returned with Becca Santini by his side. Glassover's ad hoc Slack lesson wasn't finished, but Mayer turned to Santini.

"Ms. Santini, I'm Captain Kelly Mayer, Montgomery County Police. I understand you use a communications tool called Slack."

Santini did a quick side to side glance. "Yes, it's great."

Makes one of us, Glassover said to herself.

"And it's Mrs. Santini. My husband is Italian, capisce?"

Mayer smiled. "Capito, Mrs. Santini. I'm Kelly Costanzo Mayer."

That warmed Santini's smile. Mayer continued, "Does everyone in the building have access to Slack by using their cell phones?"

"Yes. My team asked for that when the system was rolled out. We try to get everyone to use it, but like any new piece of tech the acceptance is a bit slow."

"OK, but is there a way I can send a message via a private channel . . ." Mayer looked at Glassover to be sure she was using the correct terminology.

Glassover nodded with a "keep going" expression on her face.

"I want to start and maintain a specific topic of conversation going," Mayer said, working off the knowledge she gleaned from Glassover regarding how Slack works.

"OK, so we need to create a unique channel in Slack. One where everyone can search a term to find out the latest news," Santini said.

She could tell this was unfamiliar turf to Captain Mayer. "It's like a hashtag on Twitter, only its visibility is limited to people in a group."

"And can I create a group that is basically everyone in that building?" Mayer asked.

"One already exists," Santini said as she punched up the #everyone group on Slack.

"I see where you're going," Mayer said. "Let's say something like . . . ."

Joe Barron and Steve Donelson remained huddled with their coworkers on the floor around a large conference table when their phones began to buzz. Each had a different tone, set to each person's preference for notifications that messages have come in.

"Slack," Donelson and Barron said, almost simultaneously.

"It's from Becca Santini?" Donelson said, looking down at his phone.

"The Data Master herself," Barron said, invoking a nickname Santini loathed. "But the message says it isn't from her."

Everyone read the message on their phones in silence. Miller looked over Barron's shoulder to read his phone.

> "This is Captain Kelly Mayer, Montgomery County Police. I am temporarily using Becca Santini's Slack account to speak with everyone privately."

"Great, we're getting a 'We regret to tell you you're all gonna die' message via Slack. How very 21st Century," Donelson said.

"Steve, shut the fuck up, and let us take this in, willya?" Barron said, never once looking from his phone.

"I second that. Steve, please shut up for a minute," Miller said.

Donelson was a bit shocked that mild-mannered Dorothy Miller just told him to shut up.

"We're all under a lot of pressure here, Steve," Miller added, clearly seeing Donelson's reaction to her words.

Barron was busy reading the message, which said:

> "By now you know there is an active shooter incident underway in the Trask building. Please be aware that the police are on site in force and are, as you read this, moving through the building and will help you evacuate. In the meantime, PLEASE DO NOT MOVE IF YOU ARE IN A SECURE LOCATION. We have a high degree of confidence that we know where the shooter is. As of right now, he is not moving through the building, and neither should you unless you are accompanied by Montgomery County police officers."

The message continued:

> "As you can imagine, the switchboard at police headquarters has been flooded all morning. You are free to call us, of course, but communicating through this channel, #TraskCrisis, may be a good way to get information."

Donelson, ever the communication stickler, groaned. "Why did she have to use THAT hashtag?"

"Steve, they're flying by the seat of their pants," Barron said. "I'm impressed they are using this tool to communicate with everyone."

"Santini is going to need a new Slack account, that's for sure," Dorothy said.

The Slack message started working right away. People responded to Mayer's message, initially with some "Becca, is this really you, or is this a joke?" Mayer handled that by taking a selfie of herself with Santini and attaching that to a response.

"No smiles, Ms. Santini," Mayer said before the photo was snapped. Mayer made sure her hat was on, her badge visible, and that Santini could be fully seen. She understood that people would see the blood on Santini's right arm—she cut herself as she climbed out of her office window—and in this case that would drive home the severity of the situation. The photo would look legitimate. No one would pose with fresh blood on themselves.

"We could put something out on Twitter telling people in the building to check their Slack accounts," Officer Brown said.

"And then we risk alerting Tomlinson that we're up to something. No, thank you," Mayer responded.

Before long, people in the building started responding with more substantive messages, asking where the S.W.A.T. team was in relation to where they were hiding, whether the shooter was in custody. Mayer calmly responded—directing Santini, actually, since it was Santini's phone, and she was more adept at typing quickly.

Police, working in teams of three, were able to quickly move through the building, find employees who were in hiding, and help escort them to safety. What began as a trickle of people coming out of the north entry to the Trask building, quickly turned into a steady flow, much like watching people emerge from a jetway at an airport. Only this destination was a lot nicer and far more appreciated than a trip to luggage claim or ground transportation at just about any airport.

The three S.W.A.T. teams quickly and silently moved along the long hallways of the building. When they came upon employees huddled behind desks or just lying on the floor, they made a quick determination if anyone was injured—was there blood anywhere, basically, for this quick triage—and at the same time softly saying, "Show me your hands, NOW!" The message was delivered convincingly enough that everyone immediately obeyed.

"OK, the police say they are going door to door, knocking and escorting people out," Bannon said. The Slack messages were keeping him glued to his phone. "These instructions are coming from a Captain Mayer."

"You could Google her. She's legit," Janet, the temp service employee, said.

"Do you know how close the S.W.A.T. teams are to us?" Miller asked.

"No, but Captain Mayer said they are confident they know where the gunman is, and they are working to clear offices on the second floor. That's us."

Donelson was being unusually quiet. He nodded as Barron spoke, but not much else.

Right then there came a soft but distinct tap on the door, accompanied by a clear voice saying, "Is anybody in there?"

"That's us," Barron said. Everyone stood up except for Donelson, who was closest to the door. He didn't move.

"Steve?' Miller asked.

Donelson was still frozen in place.

We're wasting time, Barron thought. He quickly moved past and around Donelson, unlocked the conference room door and slowly opened it.

The first thing Barron saw was the angry end of a shotgun.

Shit. What did I just do?

Then he heard a voice, "Show me your hands, NOW." It was a Montgomery County Police S.W.A.T. team member. He was backed up by three other officers, all holding shields.

"Keep your hands where I can see them and come out," the S.W.A.T. officer said. His tone was firm, not threatening.

Barron exited the room first, followed by Miller, Donelson, and the others.

"Turn right, go all the way to the end of the hall, then down the stairs," the S.W.A.T. officer said. "Keep your hands above your heads, please!"

"That's just like Mayer told us in her Slack message," Donelson finally said. The five moved quickly, in a run/walk motion down the long hallway, passing a human body that was soaked in blood. *A construction worker?* Barron thought. Larry's white shirt was so soaked with blood he was unrecognizable. Barron would forever deeply regret not recognizing the body of his fallen co-worker.

A Montgomery County police officer was standing near Larry's body. "Please keep moving, and keep your hands where they can be seen," he said. They kept moving until they were outside the building. The last Montgomery County policeman they passed said the words, "It's OK. You're safe now."

This process was repeated for every door and every office in the building. A Montgomery County police officer was standing by the stairs, his shotgun in his right hand, the gunstock resting on his right hip. "Move to the door quickly. And please keep your hands above your heads." He repeated this instruction each time Trask employees came to the stairwell, occasionally adding "you're safe now." Those three words, "you're safe now," was music to the ears of someone who five minutes earlier had feared for their life or had been making peace with their maker.

A caravan of shuttle buses took employees from the Trask parking lot to one of two locations: a nearby fire department and the lobby of the MarLock Aerospace building.

Everyone got on the shuttle buses except Donelson and Barron. "Joe, we need to establish a communications center," Donelson said.

This guy. We just escaped with our lives intact and . . . Bannon stopped mid-thought. As much of a pain as Donelson could be, he was right.

"OK, where do we do that?"

"Someone just said MarLock Aerospace is offering space. Let's head there. I'm calling Ed Reisman now."

"Joe! Steve!" The voice was from Bert Schorr, who had just arrived from his aborted trip to Maryland's Eastern Shore. After a quick, "Are you guys OK?" exchange, the three of them went to MarLock Aerospace to set up a communications command post.

Not long after the first Slack message was sent, the Trask building was virtually empty of all employees. The last thing to do was to approach the conference room where Mel Tomlinson waited. The phone in the conference room where he waited rang.

"Hey."

"Hi, Mel. It's Caleb Brown. I'm here with Tara Glassover. We're right outside of the building."

"OK."

"Mel, you are going to hear a knock at the door. That'll be one of our officers. They are going to escort you from the conference room outside. OK?"

"All right."

Tomlinson's monosyllabic responses weren't giving Brown or anyone else a warm, fuzzy feeling. But the building was evacuated, and it was time to move in.

Police set up in force outside of the conference room. Kevlar suited S.W.A.T. members in front, each holding a protective ballistic shield, and uniform police backing them up. All weapons were trained on the door. The lead S.W.A.T. commander stood to the side and rapped on the metal door.

"Police. Open the door. Now."

The door slowly opened. Mel Tomlinson looked ahead, then quickly to his left and right.

"Show me your hands, NOW!" the S.W.A.T. commander said. His tone was a lot less friendly than it was with Barron and others who escaped.

Tomlinson put up both hands. Both were empty.

"Walk out slowly, then get down on your knees, please."

Tomlinson complied.

The second Tomlinson's knees hit the floor S.W.A.T. officers put restraints on his arms.

"Is Tara here?" Tomlinson said. "I said I would surrender to her."

"She's downstairs waiting to see you," the S.W.A.T. commander said. "We keep our promises."

The S.W.A.T. commander was under specific orders to speak as little as possible to Tomlinson. All other officers at that location were told to not say a word.

The team led Tomlinson down the hallway from the conference room, and down the stairs to the south entrance of the building ... opposite the entrance where all Trask employees exited.

Just inside the lobby, standing amid the broken glass, bent steel, shattered desk, and cordoned off area where security guard Carl Wilson took his final breath, stood Tara Glassover, Officer Caleb Brown, Captain Kelly Myers, and Officers LaTulipe and Drew. Tomlinson looked directly at Glassover.

"Hi, Mel. I'm Tara. We finally meet face-to-face."

"Yeah, how about that?" Tomlinson said. Then looking at the four police officers he said, "I surrender."

LaTulipe, working on direct orders from Captain Mayer, immediately began speaking, "Melvin Tomlinson, you are under arrest," he said, launching into reciting the Miranda warning:

"You have the right to remain silent. Anything you say can and will be used against you in a court of law. You have the right to an attorney. If you cannot afford an attorney, one will be provided for you. Do you understand the rights I have just read to you?"

"Yes," Tomlinson said.

"With these rights in mind, do you wish to speak to me?" LaTulipe said.

"OK," Tomlinson responded.

Glassover knew that was her opening. "Mel, why did you do this?"

At that moment the icy glare she received from Mayer could have extinguished the Sun.

"I don't know," Mel said.

That wasn't much of a response, Glassover thought.

"You murdered three people," Officer Drew said through his clenched teeth.

NOW, it's a good response, Glassover thought.

"Save it, Officer Drew," Mayer shouted as Tomlinson was put in a police car.

CRISIS LIFE CYCLE
STEP NINE—DEBRIEF

The following report was heard later that day.

"I'm Tara Glassover with WDCN radio on site at the Trask International office building in Bethesda. The building was the site of a bloody, violent mass shooting today. Three individuals are dead, and the gunman, forty-four-year-old Melvin Tomlinson is in police custody.

"According to Montgomery County Police, Tomlinson drove a late model Lincoln Navigator sport utility vehicle up the sidewalk leading to the large glass double doors at the Trask building. His SUV crashed through those doors, killing a security guard at the front desk. According to the police, Tomlinson then exited the vehicle, brandishing two guns, and began randomly shooting. He killed two other Trask employees who were fleeing for their lives. Here is Montgomery County Police Captain Kelly Mayer."

AUDIO OF CAPTAIN MAYER: "We have taken Melvin Tomlinson into custody today. He will be held at the Montgomery County lockup pending an appearance in court. I extend my thanks to the courageous work by members of the Montgomery County Police Department. I also wish to extend my personal condolences to the families of the victims, and my additional thanks to everyone who helped us bring this sad event to a conclusion."

AUDIO OF GLASSOVER: "One aspect of the story is the unusual opportunity I had to speak with Mr. Tomlinson. I was calling what I thought was the office phone of someone I know who works here for Task. Apparently, I called the wrong number, and Mr. Tomlinson answered. While he did not specifically confess to the crimes he is charged with, he did tell me that he, quote, 'shot my guns and I guess I got a few.'"

AUDIO OF MAYER: "The police truly appreciate the cooperation we received from the press, particularly the staff with

WDCN. Their assistance helped us identify where in the building Mr. Tomlinson was hiding."

AUDIO OF GLASSOVER: "I'm Tara Glassover, reporting from Bethesda."

Glassover shut the mic off and placed it in her equipment bag. A Slack message immediately came in from Marc Tilling: "Great work, Tara. You earned your keep today, LOL."

High praise from that guy, Glassover thought. She was wrapping up her equipment when Coke Stewart from WJKA was walking by after hearing her report.

"Appreciate the cooperation, eh? You got lucky," he said to Glassover.

"Yeah, how did your reporting help, Coke?"

"I'm not here to help, Tara."

"You got that right, bucko."

Stewart uttered a few curse words under his breath and walked off.

The communications team for Trask International offices in Foot and in Bethesda listened to Glassover's report.

"About as good as it can get, I suppose," Taylor said.

"She covered just about everything," Allen said. "I noticed, though, she didn't mention the names of the victims. Have the police not given that out?"

"Not yet, Geeta. We're still working with them on that matter," Reisman said. He tapped in a phone number on his phone as he spoke.

"Ed?"

"Frank, hello. Can you confirm the names of the victims?"

"Yeah, Carl Wilson, Carla Augustine, and Tom Larry. Something here about Augustine having a relative who also works for Trask?"

"That's what I was looking for. Thanks, Frank." Reisman ended that call and got Alexis Shimada on the phone next.

"Alexis, one of the victims, Carla Augustine, has a relative who works for Trask International. We need to find and notify them before her name is released."

"OK, but don't the police do that, Ed?"

"Next of kin, yes. But by my understanding, Augustine had a cousin or something like that somewhere in the company. I'd prefer if that individual didn't hear their relative's name for the first time in a news report."

"I'll find out what I can and get back to you, Ed."

"I know you will, Alexis. Thank you."

Aftermath—Justice

The wheels of justice moved as expected after Tomlinson's arrest. On June 11, he was deemed mentally incapable of standing trial and was remanded to a Maryland Department of Corrections psychiatric hospital in Jessup, Maryland. One year later, after he was re-evaluated and found mentally capable of assisting in his own defense, a trial date was set. But before a jury could be selected, Tomlinson pled guilty to three counts of murder, property damage to Trask, reckless driving, and multiple assault with a deadly weapon charges. On July 12, 2020, he was sentenced to three consecutive life in prison sentences, plus an additional 20 years for the multiple assault charges. He would die in prison.

That he did. On September 1, 2020 Mel Tomlinson fashioned a noose out of his bedsheets and hanged himself in his prison cell.

When word of Tomlinson's death reached Officer Tom Drew his only thought was, *Fine. Taxpayer dollars are no longer feeding that guy.*

A few press inquiries were directed toward Task International. Geeta Allen's only comment on behalf of the company was that justice had been served when Tomlinson was sentenced. The company would have no further comments.

On May 24, 2020 one year after the shooting, Becca Santini was in her office in Bethesda. It was her one day of the week in the office due to the COVID-19 pandemic. She was wearing a mask, even though no one was working in her area of the building. She happened to look up at the clock at 11:30 a.m. and said to herself, "Oh yeah, that's today, isn't it?" She then went back to work. Rather than 130 people trapped in offices, there were about the same number of people working remotely and needing her help. As far as Santini was concerned, that was more important than anything that happened one year ago.

THE PLANNING
Two years earlier.

TRASK INTERNATIONAL HEADQUARTERS
FOOT, NEW YORK
Office of Alexis Shimada, corporate director of human resources
May 2017

"Care for the individual means everything for running a successful business. Unappreciated employees are less productive, more likely to quit and that costs Trask International millions of dollars each year in recruitment, training, and the unmeasurable cost to profits. Blend in absenteeism, tardiness, lack of motivation, and stress-related injuries, and the cost goes well beyond having an undervalued workforce."

Alexis Shimada stopped writing to review that statement. *Well, that's textbook SHRM[4] doctrine,* she thought as she continued writing. She was adapting SHRM (Society for Human Resource Management) boilerplate to fit Trask jargon.

Shimada knew what she was writing would ultimately land in someone's desk drawer or file cabinet at best. At worst, it will land in a trash bin. It would only be reviewed when absolutely necessary, like when Trask fires an employee who then decides to lawyer up and sue the company. Trask needed to identify an accepted set of rules and make every attempt to follow them. SHRM was the best possible resource for that task.

"A worker's desire to do a good job is priceless," her notes from SHRM read. "It is one of the core components of a successful business. When workers value their ability to do good work enough to ask for guidance, for example, the manager must value that request and deal with it accordingly."

Lord, even I hate reading this, she thought as she continued writing and editing, knowing that, in addition to eventually being forgotten, whatever she wrote would go through numerous committee reviews. Sometimes it would come through unscathed. Frequently, it would come back to her for "massaging," a term the corporate review folks like to use when they say you really need to completely rewrite something.

Someday we'll need this stuff. She thought as she continued writing.

"Trask International values employees who work hard and smart. Trask has a deep-seated practice of *care for the individual*. They learn the most efficient way to complete tasks while saving time and money. We recognize and appreciate employees who show up on time, do their jobs, and are always dependable. We strive to create a work environment where employees not only know they are valued, but they are able to adapt and thrive in a forever changing and competitive business. Enthusiastic employees always create an environment of teamwork and goodwill and have a positive outlook about work."

Shimada kept reminding herself as she wrote, *Avoid negative words, like "attitude" or "terse."* She remembered something from a seminar. Employees who are being fired should never be told so using the "F" word. *Can we just say you're fucked and get it over with?* She kept those dark thoughts to herself. Instead, she wrote,

"Separation from Trask is an opportunity for the employee to explore new opportunities, new and different career paths."

She was careful to highlight and include the line "care for the individual." That was a core value of Trask that had been a part of the company since its earliest days. The phrase "care for the individual" was all around the company: in training manuals, posters, within speeches delivered by executives at annual kickoff events, even within letters of complaint from employees. "I thought 'care for the individual' was a part of this company," someone would say in a letter of complaint before launching into a rant. It was an ingrained part of the Trask company culture.

A break from Shimada's tedious wordsmithing arrived.

"Alexis, those posters you ordered are available for you to review."

The greeting was from Mary Doane, the human resources administrator for communications.

Shimada looked up from her desk. "Mary, remind me again, what posters?"

It wasn't an unreasonable request, nor was Shimada being sarcastic, although she could hold her own when it came to a tart tongue. H.R. produced dozens of posters for employee communications—reminding people when the benefits sign-up period is beginning and near the end, announcing employee events, reminders to follow specific company rules for managing confidential information, and so on.

"Sorry, Alexis. These are the safety posters for active shooter training."

"Right, Mary. Thank you. Let's see them."

Mary placed a PDF printout of the posters before Shimada. They were straightforward enough, advising employees of the three primary rules for survival in the event someone with a weapon is on the premises. That is, someone with a weapon who is actively using it; some sites have armed security.

"I suppose these are necessary, but good lord I hope we never need them," Shimada muttered to herself. She looked at the last piece of advice, coaching employees to fight. "Jesus, it shows stick figures holding a bar stool, and they're about to swing it at someone," Shimada said.

"It's the standard poster the state police in most states advise us to use," Mary said.

"It'll look great next to the 'New Vacation Policy' posters in the coffee room. Which do you think people will focus on? Especially since the first piece of advice, in big letters, is RUN."

Doane just looked down. She knew her boss had a caustic streak in her that she wasn't afraid to use it on someone.

"So, it's RUN, HIDE, FIGHT. Yeesh, try convincing someone to display these bad boys."

"We should probably include something in a cover note from you explaining these are recommended for use by local and state police," Doane said. "It might be the extra push needed to get someone to actually post them."

"Agreed, Mary. Thanks." Shimada looked at the 24-by-18-inch poster, then added, "I think the break rooms everywhere are going to need bigger bulletin boards, don't you?"

CRISIS PLANNING SESSION

TRASK CORPORATE HEADQUARTERS
FOOT, NEW YORK
DECEMBER 2016

Ed Reisman did a quick headcount on the room. Two regional communications managers—Joyce Eli and Burt Schorr, Alexis Shimada from human resources, Bonnie Dekker from IT, Sylvester Moore from marketing, and Ron Reynolds from legal.

"Good morning. I know it's a cliché, but thanks for finding time in your busy schedules to be here. We gathered to work on a plan that none of us hopes we will ever have to use: a crisis communications plan we would use in the event of work stoppages or unforeseen interruptions."

Reisman was a Certified Crisis Management Certified Planner (CMCP)[5], which may sound vague but holds an important distinction. He studied crisis management through the Business Continuity Management Institute, which runs extensive, comprehensive, and difficult training on becoming CMCP certified. In other words, it's an acronym he didn't just pay to have on his resume. This certification adds a sense of gravitas to the argument that crisis planning should take place in any enterprise.

The CMCP training also helped Reisman be objective when considering human behavior during a crisis planning situation. The biggest challenge, of course, is getting people to think about something they either never think of, or they put off thinking about it, like some people put off going to a doctor.

Everyone in the room already knew Reisman would preach how crisis communications planning is not just planning. It's creating a partnership between people who normally do very little together, even though they all work for the same company. It comprises talking about a lot of scenarios—some having at best a remote possibility of ever happening, others being downright crazy—for a company the size of Trask International to manage. The job is getting everyone to continuously think seriously about what-if scenarios.

There was a lot to cover, so Reisman thought it best to compartmentalize things. He liked calling it "McNuggettizing:" Cover material in short bites and use lots of breaks. *People may feel less like we're dragging them through a meaningless procedure if I can maintain interest and get involved*, he thought. He would try to break the training up into specific segments:

1. Who leads the crisis response?
2. What are the types of crises the company could face?
3. What general messages should be developed, and how should they be adjusted on the fly?
4. Understanding how to deal with the press; they can be your friend and your enemy.

WHO LEADS THE CRISIS RESPONSE?

For a large company like Trask International, the leadership fell to multiple persons. Legal, human resources and facilities, and communications were logical candidates.

Communications would take the lead on writing messages *in conjunction with* departments like legal, human resources, and others as deemed necessary. The communications team would also manage all social media accounts and—this is the tricky part—in some cases, depending on the severity of a crisis, may need to post messages to social media *without checking with all parties*. Reisman knew that would be a topic of discussion, for sure.

Legal also plays a big role here. It's one thing to have a public face talking about the crisis, but whatever that public face says needs to be in line with company legal parameters. Reisman made sure Reynolds knew his role was integral.

Human resources, too, is a critical part of the team. If employees are hurt, then what and how much is said depends a lot on H.R. parameters. There were Trask locations where members of the same family worked. A lot of people could be negatively affected in the event of a business interruption.

Shimada's plate of responsibilities also included facility management. Most buildings where Trask International personnel could be found were leased, but the responsibility of working with site management, putting furniture in offices, ensuring wiring was up to spec, fell on her.

This hydra-headed leadership approach could be cumbersome, but for Trask, it worked. More than who had what responsibility, Reisman, Reynolds, and Shimada worked well together, even if they did not always get along. They were also smart enough to know other role players would have responsibilities in the event of a crisis. For example, customer support, project engineering, and community relations could easily become central players in a crisis response. A very bad crisis can interrupt support for customers. A product failure would require careful analysis of product development and rollout, and if the crisis was big enough, it could close operations, and a community can be severely negatively affected. Every day on his way to work, Reisman passed a Dunkin' Donuts gas station and convenience store. Imagine how they'd be hurt if a significant crisis closed local Trask International operations for a time.

JOE DIORIO | 129

WHAT TYPES OF CRISES COULD THE COMPANY FACE?

Next, Trask needed a plan to confirm the facts of a crisis—which means straightforward inquiries to first responders and/or contacts at an incident. It means identifying and training team members who manage response and manage how the company responds to press inquiries, the tsunami of social media posts that will inevitably come about after a crisis—"false news" is how the Massachusetts Institute of Technology's Media Lab will call it[6]—although no one used the term that day. A 2018 study by researchers Soroush Vosoughi, Sinan Aral, and Deb Roy—looking at tweets related to the 2013 Boston Marathon bombing—finds that negative news traveled throughout social media 70 times faster than good news. It also generated false (not fake) news headlines.

This surprising flow of bad news riding a fast horse can affect how a business enterprise reacts. If the news is overwhelming, some companies may try to roll up the proverbial sidewalks, not respond to press, customer, or even employee inquiries. Logically, what happens then is the negative news just takes on a life of its own. The news business hates a vacuum, and in the absence of facts, some will get made up.

The process to combat this requires more than just a media reaction plan. Stakeholders—employees, customers, investors—need to know the business understands the challenges the crisis presents and is capable of responding to it.

Saying that is easy. Getting a room full of executives to agree upon a plan of action is a little trickier. Not impossible. Just tricky.

And perhaps the biggest hurdle is managing one's way through a crisis. A plan is one thing, working when the plan has to be put into action is another. Reisman thought a lot about that line attributed to boxer Mike Tyson: "Everybody has a plan 'til they are punched in the mouth." For Trask International, that means prepared statements will undoubtedly need to be changed at the spur of the moment without review by the bullet-proof bureau-cracy of Trask International weighing in on every comma that is removed or added. A company not accustomed to granting autonomy needed to do that in the event of a crisis. It was going to be a big topic of discussion today.

Media relations, internal and external messaging, social media, managing the unexpected. Obviously, crisis planning is a big iceberg.

To demonstrate this, he had prepared planning documents that helped make the workload palatable. The documents ex-plained that a crisis can fall into one of four categories.

Level 1: The highest level of crisis. Something that completely disrupts business. A fire, a company-wide cyber-attack, an active shooter at a Trask International building. Something that makes the business grind to a halt.

Level 2: Something like a large power outage, fire, or damage to one or two business sites. The planning documents call this "a moderate risk," but Reismann kept that language out of today's meeting, fearing it sounded far too clinical. *Let us avoid any dis-traction*, he thought.

Level 3: A situation that can cause a long-term risk. The death of an executive or say a team of employees is killed in an accident. That happened to IBM in 1985 when Don Estridge, considered the "father" of the IBM Personal Computer, was killed when a Delta Airlines flight crashed at Dallas/Fort Worth International Airport. The personal computer business at IBM employed 10,000 people at the time, and legitimate questions were raised about the future of that line of business.

Level 4: Most crises fall into this category. They're slightly bigger problems than normal. A fire, a water main that breaks and temporarily shuts down an office building.

In each of these cases, there are roles, responsibilities, and jobs to do to keep the business running. Everyone in the room—press people, human resources, legal—had a role to play.

WHAT GENERAL MESSAGES SHOULD BE DEVELOPED, AND HOW CAN THEY BE ADJUSTED ON THE FLY?

Best way to do this is dive right in, he thought.

"OK, let's begin," Reisman said. "For starters, who caught the typo on page one of my briefing paperwork?"

The room fell silent. Everyone started looking down at their copy of Reisman's papers, which he distributed via email a week before. Everyone, that is, except Joyce Eli, communications manager for the Northeast and Central states. She stared at Reisman and said, "Ed, there is no typo on the first page."

"Can't be sure of that, Joyce," Schorr said as he continued to scan page one.

"Yes, I can, Burt. I read the whole thing. There is no typo."

"And for that, Joyce wins a prize," Reisman said, handing Eli a $50 Starbucks gift card.

Everyone caught on. Reisman was running a test to see who really did read the briefing materials.

"Ah, SNEAK-EEE," Shimada said.

"Now that I have everyone's attention, we can begin," Reisman said. He went on to explain what everyone in the room probably knew: crisis planning is preparing for the worst, hoping for the best, and being willing to hear someone say, "See? I told you we didn't need to do this."

He wrote a few broad-brush guidelines on the white board:

Ensure that everyone is safe.

Show compassion.

Be responsive to customers (directly or via a third-party i.e.—the press).

Keep the business on track.

"Whatever we do, these should be the things we keep in mind," Reisman said, adding, "Anyone disagree?" Everyone shook their heads to indicate they didn't.

"OK, then let's talk specifics, beginning with a Level One situation. Perhaps a remote possibility, like a flood or tornado at a Trask International property. Suppose a natural disaster occurs at one of our buildings. Enough damage happens to shut that operation down. Worse yet, damage happens when someone is in the building and people get hurt or are trapped."

Reisman saw Reynolds raise his eyebrows and look down at his notepad. He continued unabated. "I know it's highly unlikely, but bear with me. Let's talk about what our communications should look like if there is a natural disaster at one of our properties."

"Just refer everything to the police and first responders," Reynolds said, without looking up.

"That's a part of what we do, yes. But there is more to it than that. Do we need to confirm what's happening? If so, how? Do we need to know how many people work in that specific building? Is there any damage to our day-to-day operations?"

"A tornado could hit one of our cloud computing centers in the Southeastern United States," Schorr chimed in. "How many customer computer screens go blank if that happens?"

Reynolds looked at Schorr. "Go blank?"

"Customers rely on our data centers for their day-to-day operations," Schorr said.

"Don't they have backups?" Reynolds asked.

"Sure. Their backup is usually a Trask International data center," Dekker chimed in. "But in the scenario Ed is talking about, one of those backups could be compromised."

"Exactly," Reisman said. Dekker gave him a good opening. "I'd like us to think about how we go about confirming what is happening. How, or do, we communicate with customers? Who is the person who interfaces with the authorities? Should all calls go to one person?" The hard part about what Reisman was doing was to explain without sounding preachy.

"Remember, too, we have lots of properties in the country," said Schorr. "Some house a hundred or more people ... people who have families, who spend money in the neighborhood where their office work is. They're a part of a community, and something bad happening can have a profound impact on more than just Trask."

"So, a bad thing that happens in one place has a ripple effect on all locations," Reisman said.

"We shouldn't speak for the police," Reynolds said. He still wasn't looking up.

"You're right, Ron, and we won't do that." Reisman knew the value of keeping people engaged rather than reacting to a brusque comment with one of his own. "But if people are trapped in a building because part of it collapsed due to a tornado, then someone's spouse, partner, kids, and friends will want to know what's happening. We can at least say we are working with the police."

"That's all we should say," Reynolds said.

"I am sure everyone agrees, Ron. But let's make sure our message is consistent and our actions help the overall recovery process." Reisman could tell he was making little progress. Reynolds was trained to be risk averse. The less said in the event of a crisis, the better. Reynolds' recalcitrance could be endemic. He knew there would be the need for convincing, and he had his case ready.

"Everyone, please. If there is a crisis at one building, say an office in Atlanta, it's possible that a local TV in Raleigh or Cincinnati or any city where we have an office is going to go on site in Raleigh or Cincinnati to do reports about security and day-to-day life at Trask offices in their neighborhoods."

"And if they can't get inside, they'll just stand outside to do person on the street interviews," Schorr chimed in.

"Correct," Reisman continued. "If we want to just say we are aware of the situation, and we are working with first responders, that's fine. But I think it is beneficial that every Trask International manager at every office in the country understands what is going on and what Trask International's position is."

"There's an efficient way we can do that," Dekker said. She briefly explained that Trask International was implementing Slack as a messaging system throughout the company. "Enterprise-wide" is the terminology she used. Slack is messaging via specific channels. It allows for more efficient communication among teams. "We can create a channel for regional managers and one for everyone who works in a specific location. It's just a more efficient communication tool. It's also going to be available on everyone's phones." It would take time to implement the system company-wide, but it was an important step to maintain consistent internal communications.

"Everyone's phone? Even people who don't have phones paid for by Trask?" Reisman said.

"Yes," Dekker responded.

"So, are we now paying for everyone's phone?" Shimada asked. She already knew the answer. Trask International pays for the phones for people in sales and consulting positions, but not for anyone else. It was her personal craw that stuck in her side. Trask International employees were asked to work from home, yet the company didn't pay for anyone's home internet connection. Shimada didn't agree with this position, but she figured it was not a hill to die on.

"OK, so for now, let's say we have an efficient internal communication tool in Slack. It could be what we use to share the company crisis incident holding statement," Reisman said.

"Ed, tell me again what a holding statement is," Shimada asked.

"Let's call it a wish on paper," Reisman said. "It's something we want everyone connected with Trask to know and be able to share with the media and with customers should the need arise. Wherever they work, our employees are the front line of communications to the world during a crisis. It's possible they will interact directly not just with the press but with customers who are interested primarily in how this crisis—whatever it is—affects their business with us. Part of our planning today is to make sure our employees know what to say should negative news or feedback come through the door."

"The story, or a story, is going to get told whether we are involved or not. It's better if we are involved," said Eli. She worked with the press in New York. More than anyone else in the room, she was familiar with the unique proclivities of the media.

The room was silent after Reisman's monologue. "Let's just talk for now. We're not on any clock," Reisman added.

The team worked on the standby statement. The first draft of the first statement they crafted was relatively straightforward.

Trask is aware of a [insert disaster] at [INSERT BUILDING/ SITE INFORMATION]. We are working with the local police [INSERT NAME OF LOCAL POLICE DEPARTMENT] and will have no further comment at this time.

"Wait," said Eli. "Can we be less abrupt than saying 'we have no further comment'? Just saying we have no further comment could be taken as confrontational, and it's better to be as non-confrontational as possible."

"What if we changed the end of the statement to, "at this point, any statement we make would not be helpful,'" Dekker suggested. She worked closely with Reisman and had a good knack for public relations.

"Not helpful … how?" Reisman asked. "Just tell me what your thought is with phrasing it that way."

"I'm thinking we want to make it clear we aren't saying anything because we don't want to interfere with what the police—or whatever first responders are involved—are doing. There's time later to make further statements," Dekker explained. "Sure, it's a cover-our-butt statement, but this might minimize follow-up questions from the press."

"What if you say you are working with the police, and they are the ones you should talk to," Reynolds added.

At last, a helpful statement out of Ron Reynolds, Reisman thought. *Now let's see if we can get something on paper. Not just something Ron and the other lawyers agree with, but something that's of value.* One of the bigger challenges in crisis planning is that you have to work with others as part of a team whether you like that individual or not.

Reisman felt they had the working parts of a standby statement. This message can be slightly modified for initial "talking points"—a rough public script that a public relations person can follow to ensure they stay on message during news media interviews—for the Trask press office.

"OK, great," Reisman said. "So, what if we go with . . ."

Trask is aware of a [insert disaster] at our office building at [ADDRESS]. We are working with first responders, who are the primary source of information about the incident.

"OK, we know what the external tweet is," Reisman continued. "I strongly suggest we make the internal message almost identical."

"Well, if you are 'strongly suggesting it,' " Shimada said. A rare wry smile came out.

"Thank you. Our employees are all over Twitter, but we still need to tell them the same thing. Are there any additions or deletions we want to make here?"

"Depending on the circumstances, we may need to suggest that everyone refrain from contacting the location. If there is a fire, flood, or something even worse, people will only upset themselves if they try to call friends who work at the site in question," Dekker said.

"We can suggest it, but I doubt anyone will follow that recommendation," Schorr said.

"Agreed," Reisman said. He wanted to get this part of the discussion done quickly. "But we're doing our jobs if we do make that recommendation."

"So how about we say ..." Amazingly, the following suggestion came from Reynolds.

Trask is aware of the [insert disaster] at our office building at [ADDRESS]. We are working with the local police, who are the primary source of information about the incident. At this time, we ask employees not to try and contact anyone they may know at that site as it may negatively compromise the first responder operation.

"We need to make it a thread message, Ed," Schorr said. "Add links in the thread to information on a web page. That way we can 'pin' it to the top of our Twitter profile."

"Good thought, Burt. Thank you," Reisman said, smiling because the ideas were now proliferating throughout the group.

With Twitter having a character message limit, the statement would have to be tweeted in multiple parts. But it was a working agreement nevertheless.

After lunch, the matter of social media was next on the list. This was not going to be easy. Reisman knew that a story—positive or negative—can take on a life of its own when the business enterprise does nothing during a crisis. That problem becomes exponentially larger with social media.

"OK, next on the agenda is understanding and deciding what we do with social media," Reisman started. "And to cut anyone off at the pass ... doing nothing simply is not an option."

The group discussed in general terms how negative news seems to travel faster than good news, especially on social media. Eventually, their suspicions would prove true. In 2018, the MIT Media Lab[6] would take a serious look at this subject. Just by casual observance, MIT scientists noticed that negative news surrounding the 2013 bombing of the Boston Marathon rapidly outpaced positive news. Further research demonstrated some hard realities. The MIT Media Lab guys found bad news travels along social media six times faster than good news. And that rate of speed is pushed by people, not the so-called automated "bots" that falsely inflate some individuals' follower count or spread news. No, people seem to be genuinely fixated on bad news, and they will pass it along, comment on it, and criticize someone far faster than compliment.

Therefore, Reisman decided there was truth to another old adage, "A satisfied customer tells one person, whereas a dissatisfied customer tells everyone they know."

Geeta Allen joined the meeting to provide an overview of the collection of social media monitoring tools to keep on top of what is being said and reported. She explained how Google Alerts, HootSuite, and Sprout Social could monitor what is being tweeted about Trask International, and how a tool called Answer the Public can provide very precise search parameters people are using when going online to look up information about anything, although in this case, her efforts would be learning what people are asking about Trask International.

"That could be a lot of information you have to sift through," Reynolds said.

"It is, but we have become adept at searching for very specific terms ... bad company, negative experience, avoid working with, that kind of thing," she explained. "We won't have to respond to every single tweet, but we will have a good idea as to what people are saying about us."

"Man, I really hope we don't have to do a search like this," Reynolds said. He was mostly thinking out loud when he said that.

"Me, too," said Reisman.

"This can be an important resource," Allen explained. "There is some research from academia suggesting that social media is a primary source for news among the 18 to 35-year-old set." She was thinking of research from academics who argue that social media must be a primary source of news for that age group. That would explain why that specific age group—a group that insists they don't read newspapers or watch the evening news—are able to enjoy streaming content like *Last Week Tonight* with John Oliver or *Full Frontal* with Samantha Bee. They would have to stay abreast of the news, or they wouldn't get the humor that is such an integral part of those programs.[8] But that is a lot to explain, so Allen just left off by saying young people get their news from Twitter.

"I have a question," Joyce said. "We have been using the same image of the Trask International logo on our social media accounts for a while. Can't we freshen it up with something different?"

"We could, but that would be detrimental to our social media efforts," Allen said.

"How so?"

"A consistent image is something that will resonate with people as they scroll through social media posts. In the unlikely event of a crisis, we want someone recognizing our social media handles immediately," Allen explained. "We have built up a level of familiarity using that logo and nothing else."

She could sense her answer wasn't sitting well. "Twitter allows for banner images, the larger pictures or graphics that appear next to or behind the profile picture. THAT we can change up. Perhaps create a rotation of images."

The compromise Allen offered seemed to work for now.

Reisman decided to try a Baby Boomer reference to help Allen's argument. "Anyone here old enough to remember Howard Johnson restaurants?" Joyce, Schorr, and Dekker nodded. "Good. Remember how those restaurants all had that bright orange roof? There was a reason for that. A tired motorist driving along the Lincoln Highway or elsewhere would immediately recognize a HoJo's as a good place to get a bite to eat."

Joyce nodded. "Ever been to a Stuckey's? They did that, too."

"I could go for a Stuckey's Pecan Roll right about now," Schorr said to no one in particular.

"Let's focus, people," Reisman chided the group.

"Ah, nuts," Schorr said. It was a lame joke on the Stuckey's Pecan Roll treat, but it still elicited a brief chuckle.

"That's why we have a consistent image on our social media pages. We want to help the motorists on the Twitter highway find us."

Reisman turned to Allen, thanked her for her time.

"The really important thing to remember is that we may have to write and post a tweet or other social media posts without getting the approval of everyone and their dog. I need to hear that you are all comfortable with that," he said.

No one spoke. Again.

"We agreed that human resources, legal, and communications would take the lead on crisis communications. But in the case of a crisis, in the heat of the moment if you will, it may not be possible to have all three review social posts in advance. If the timing allows for all of us to review something, then fine. But there may be a situation where we have to tweet a message about real estate without having the head of real estate and facilities review it. That's just the nature of the beast."

There was a slight chuckle that resonated throughout the room.

"What? What am I missing?" Reisman said.

"Your real estate person is on the core team, Ed," Shimada said, softly chuckling.

Reisman looked down, let out a sigh, and smiled. "OK, folks. You got me this time. But you all understand what I am saying, right?"

Silence.

"RIGHT?"

"Gotcha, Ed," Dekker replied.

UNDERSTAND HOW TO DEAL WITH THE PRESS; THEY CAN BE YOUR FRIEND AND YOUR ENEMY

"OK, let's talk Q&As," Reisman said, moving the discussion to create a set of questions that may (or may not) be asked—by the press, by curious onlookers, by customers, and others—during a crisis. "What's one of the first questions a reporter may ask us?"

"How many people work in the building," Schorr said. "If there is any kind of shutdown or interruption of operations, then that's going to be top of everyone's mind."

"Agreed," Eli said.

"OK, then do we say how many people work in a specific location?" Reisman asked.

"No. General terms only," Shimada said.

"Wait, what the heck does that even mean?" Eli said. "The press I deal with want specifics, not generalities."

Looking straight ahead, and not at anyone, Shimada said, "If we start answering specific questions about personnel, then we are on step one of a slippery slope."

"There's nothing specific about how many people work in a building," Schorr said. "Look, you can talk to a commercial real estate agent, who can easily guestimate how many people can work in a given office space."

"Fine. Let them talk to a realtor then," Shimada said, still not looking at anyone.

"Alexis, if we do that, then a random third party is coming into the picture and telling the story for us," Reisman said, trying to keep the meeting productive and keep any and all contentious comments out. It is hard enough to get people to do crisis communications planning. People are taking time from a busy schedule to make plans for something that may never happen. Try selling THAT idea to any overworked professional.

But Reisman did sell it, and he didn't want the meeting to break down over real or imagined turf battles. "The more outside players become involved, then the greater the chance that we lose control of the narrative. We certainly don't want a random commercial realtor telling the press that a building we currently lease has—or potentially has—safety and security exposures because they know of problems at a similar property, do we? A reporter could talk to someone who knows nothing about our properties and that person may just make up their own story."

Everyone nodded, except Shimada.

"Alexis, I'd really like to know what you think," Reisman said.

"Me, too. Honest," Schorr added.

Shimada agreed. "I don't want a third party talking for Trask."

Reisman thought of a compromise. "Ron, couldn't we say how many people a building is *configured* to accommodate? We're not giving away any secrets that way."

Reynolds thought for a second, then agreed.

"Besides," Shorr chimed in, "my building's dimensions and capacity are a part of the local chamber of commerce's website . . . the part where they brag about different businesses in town. There are no secrets here." He was thinking about a brochure and website from the Potomac Area Chamber of Commerce that lauded the design of the Trask building in Bethesda where he worked, calling it a "lovely blend of old and new." He thought that was a good way of saying the building is long in the tooth but is still really nice.

TRASK INTERNATIONAL
CRISIS PLANNING BY CUSTOMER RELATIONS
JANUARY 2017

Several weeks after Ed Reisman's planning session, Sylvester Moore implemented his own planning for customer relations.

The Trask International customer relations program comprises a mix of sales, technical, and human resources employees. It was headed up by Moore, Trask International's SVP of marketing.

After attending the December 2016 crisis communications planning session, and with some additional cajoling from Bert Reisman and Alexis Shimada, Moore decided to call a meeting of the various departments representing Trask's customer relations outreach to discuss crisis planning with respect to the impact a crisis may have on customer relations.

It wasn't just Reisman and Shimada that motivated Moore. He was more impressed with research from a report from McKennon Consulting[9], the big research and Fortune 500 consulting firm, which spelled out actions a company can take in crisis planning that could directly support customers. The McKennon recommendations spelled out precise steps a business could take. "Actions speak louder than words," was a phrase Moore liked. He was drawn to logical, well thought out actions over "we gotta do something" knee-jerk reactions.

The McKennon report outlined, in detail, specific actions a business can and should do for customers in the event of a crisis:

1. Minimize risk—whatever you do, be sure it minimizes a customer's negative impact. Be sure to clearly communicate any actions with your customers.

2. Ease up on the red tape—do something with your portfolio of products and/or services that makes it even easier for customers to do business with you.

3. Be pragmatic in your actions—don't just say you will be easier to work with during the crisis ... you need to really walk the talk and be easier to work with. Be prepared, too, that some of the emergency actions you take can become permanent.

4. Maintain constant contact with customers—call them. Don't wait to be called.

5. Remain accessible at all times—for Moore, that means temporarily closing down Trask International's automated customer service lines. He would open that up for discussion, just to make things look democratic, but his mind was made up.

6. Demonstrate empathy—call a customer to ask how they are doing. Develop some deep inquiries—a decision tree, if you will—that enables Trask International customer service professionals to be absolutely sure customers are doing well.

Even if this is all bullshit, we look good in the process, Moore said to himself. The trick with today's meeting was to put his ideas into action and make it look like a group decision.

"Thanks for attending, everyone," Moore said. He knew attendance was mandatory, but a modicum of humble pie goes a long way. "Our friends in corporate communications have been putting a lot of work into crisis planning for Trask International and they have convinced me to do likewise for customer relations." He went on to discuss the McKennon recommendations, then opened the floor to a "can we do something similar" set of discussions.

"Let's talk about these recommendations. Are there any concrete actions we can take, for the purpose of customer relations?" Moore asked. The answers were boilerplate, but the discussion was moving. That was Moore's biggest objective.

"Just tell customers this is happening."

"Would it make sense to model some of the messages after whatever the corporation is saying?"

"Yes," Moore said, "but let's not let us fall into the trap of just doing whatever corporate is doing. They're speaking for the entire company. We're talking to customers." He made a mental note to have a conversation with Geeta Allen to make sure customer service social media stood out.

Moore's team settled on something more straightforward: tell customers about the crisis, identify areas of the business that may need to be adjusted to make working with Trask International easier during the crisis, and maintain a personal touch throughout the event.

The biggest discussion was around turning off automation on Trask International's customer service lines. "We're basically turning our internal teams into a giant help desk," one person complained. "We have customers using us for servers, their own IT 'back rooms.' We would be buried under calls."

"I know. I get it," Moore said, trying to allow just enough discussion but not enough to derail his objective. "Look, if we have what Ed Reisman says is a Level 1 crisis—the shit has really hit the fan—then a lot of our operations may be shut down, albeit temporarily. Rather than having someone with Trask International answer the phone and solve whatever problem a customer is calling about, we can simply be there to talk to them . . . even just take a message."

"Will that even make a difference, Sylvester?" asked Carl Ransome, regional sales manager for Trask International's Mid-Atlantic region.

"Carl, have you ever been stuck at an airport and just wish you could talk to someone with the airline you're flying? Even if that person could just say, 'Your guess is as good as mine?' That can make all the difference in the world from a peace of mind standpoint."

Ransome thought about Moore's comment before acquiescing. "Point taken, Sly. Thanks."

The discussion continued for the next hour or so, solidifying Moore's already thought-out plans.

MONTGOMERY COUNTY SCHOOL DISTRICT CRISIS PLANNING SESSION NOVEMBER 2017

Montgomery County School Superintendent William Major was the last to arrive at the meeting. Waiting for him were Michelle "Shelly" Keys, the director of communications for the school district, and George Fox, director of security for the school district.

"Sorry, folks. Too many demands on my time and not enough hours in the day . . . or however that old saying goes."

"No problem, Bill," Keys said.

Fox nodded. *Let's get on with this,* was his thought.

"We have spent a good deal of time by committee worrying about our crisis planning; that's what the active shooter drills we run are all about. We also need to settle on our crisis communications, specifically any social media messages. So I don't want to burn any more time on anyone's calendar," Major said. "Can I just see what the proposed tweets are that we use in the event we have to quickly implement a school lockdown?"

Keys punched a few keys on her laptop, and the image from her Google Doc was projected on the monitor in the conference room.

Don't hand him paper, Keys thought. *You'll never see it again and you'll never get an answer.*

The text read:

"We are aware of police activity nearby at [NAME OF SCHOOL]. Because of the sensitive nature of the incident, we are acting out of an abundance of caution, and we are putting [NAME OF SCHOOL] on a soft lockdown. That means no one enters or leaves the building until further notice."

Major stared at the screen for a few minutes, then looked at Fox. "Thoughts?"

"Why are we doing this, again?"

Keys felt her back stiffen. *This guy.*

"We need to communicate quickly with parents, businesses, and the news media, George. Like it or not, social media is the fastest way to do that."

"We could do nothing and transfer any phone calls to you, George," Keys offered, using a tone of voice so thick it could be cut with a knife.

"No thank you," Fox replied with a chuckle. "I'm just trying to stay on top of things."

"I'll help you along," Keys added, looking down at her keyboard. *Avoid eye contact lest he sees how much you dislike him.*

Major paid them no attention, turned to the screen and read aloud. "We are aware of police activity … No. Everyone will be aware of police activity. That'll be why they're checking Twitter…"

"Or calling me," Fox said, giving Keys a friendly nudge. Keys resisted the urge to shout and tell Fox to keep his hands and elbows to himself.

"And I don't want to say if an incident is sensitive or not. It could be, but let's not give anyone reason to ask questions. The whole reason we're doing this is to minimize speculation, reduce the number of questions we get, and keep parents or our business partners from going off halfcocked."

"So let's change it up a bit," Keys said. "What about…"

Sample Twitter Statement from the Goose Goslin High School Twitter Account:

Montco School generic tweet

> Montgomery County police are responding to a situation reported at an office building adjacent to our campus. Details are unconfirmed, but as a precaution, we are under a soft lockdown at this time.

"We need to explain to everyone in the school district that they should refer to a central source for information," Mayer said. "I don't want our principals, faculty, or staff making up their own stories."

"Internal messages directing everyone to refer to the school social media accounts for more information. Maybe even tell the schools to provide that direction to parents long before there is a crisis," Keys said. "I can also pin this message to the top of our Twitter feed with a link to appropriate websites."

"Right. Let's start announcing snow days on social media, too. We need to put our shoulder into making Twitter the primary tool we use for communications."

MONTGOMERY COUNTY POLICE DEPARTMENT
CRISIS PLANNING - CONFERENCE ROOM
June 2018

"OK, let's get down to this," Commander Tim Lopez said. A group of seven officers were present, including Sergeant Brenda Conner, the department's designated public information officer (PIO), and Annie Lewis, owner of LewisComm Public Relations.

"We want to have our communications ducks in a row in the event of an active shooter situation," Lopez said. He almost said, "unlikely event" but he knew better.

"Like it or not, social media is a part of our world. It's how many, probably most, people get their news. We utilize the news to tell the public about potentially dangerous situations. That can happen via a press conference but, like I said, the ground rules are changing. We need to be ready to utilize social media quickly and effectively."

He continued. "Someone has to write a tweet then send it. That requires someone at a computer or a phone while the crisis is underway."

"And if I can interject here, it's a whole lot easier to have your messages written in advance of a crisis, leaving the need to make only modifications," said Lewis.

"Correct," Lopez said, putting himself back in the conversation and giving Lewis a *when I say it's your turn* look. He knew this kind of contingency planning is hard in the best circumstances. Getting a bunch of cops to do it on a sunny afternoon when there is no crisis is going to be even harder.

"I don't want our department doing some on-the-spot scrambling to come up with a tweet that helps protect the public in the event of an active shooter or some other crisis. So, Ms. Lewis is going to lead this planning session. Annie."

Lewis stood and thanked the Commander. "Like he said, let's not waste time. First, it's important that I say this is a brainstorming session. That means there are no bad suggestions. One idea can help build upon and lead to other ideas.

"So, let's start. Our scenario is this: there is an active shooter in a grocery store. Say a Safeway on Wisconsin Avenue. What would comprise the first tweet we send out to the public?"

"Keep the fuck away from the Wisconsin Avenue Safeway," Officer Tom Drew suggested, tongue planted firmly in his cheek. Not unexpected, the reaction was a mix of chuckles and a few sighs.

Lewis smiled, looked down. "I did say there are no bad suggestions."

Commander Lopez wasn't laughing. "If I recall, Officer Drew, you wanted this to be over quickly. Your 'helpful' comments aren't going to shorten the session, are they?"

"Sorry, sir, Ms. Lewis. I couldn't resist that one."

"It's OK. We DO want people to keep their distance, so you're on the right track. 'Stay clear' is one of our messages," Lewis said as she wrote those two words on the white board.

"No bad ideas," said Drew as he gave the officer seated next to him a friendly elbow nudge.

That's where it started. The genesis of a tweet informing the public that there was danger at hand and that they should stay clear. The others in the room quickly caught on.

"Tell the public *where* the danger is. Describe it in terms of traffic, the way traffic reports on the radio do."

"Give a time stamp to the tweets. Don't rely on Twitter to do the timestamping."

"Make it abundantly clear that there is clear and present danger. We're not kidding."

"What about informing the news media where and when updates will take place?"

"Yes, but make it clear those are update sessions for credentialed press only. We don't want these update sessions to be a mob scene."

This process continued for about an hour. The results were crafted into a series of ready-to-use tweets. The intention was to make it easier for the police to inform the public, maintain public safety, all while doing their jobs and not thinking about what they should tweet. The final products would go into Sergeant Conner's "EmergencySitTweets" folder.

After a break, Lewis made a slight change to the topic. "OK, so people won't just look at their phones. Some are going to punch in the number of the police department here and start asking questions. Do we want to have some standby statements available?"

Drew thought about saying, *How about leave us the hell alone*, when he caught Commander Lopez glaring at him. The teacher always watches the class clown.

After a momentary silence, Lewis spoke up. "I'm thinking it may be beneficial to have consistent messaging. People who look at Twitter will get the same message as someone calling us—excuse me—calling YOU on the phone."

"Are we comfortable using a variation of those tweets we just agreed upon?" Sergeant LaTulipe asked.

"Sure," Lewis replied. "What do others think?"

There was a general sense of agreement around the room, interrupted by Commander Lopez. "Are you agreeing because you agree? Or are you agreeing because you want to get this the hell over with? Because I can call you back on another day to work on this."

"No, sir. Consistency makes sense," Officer Drew said. "Do we just use the same phrase or is it modified?"

Lewis was relieved. Her main tormentor seemed to be on board. "They would be mostly the same. Let's look at it from the standpoint of someone calling the police department and asking what the hell is going on at the Safeway?"

She continued, "Remember, whatever the media source—WJKA news, the newspaper, or social media—you need to own the story. Do not rely on someone else to tell the story because they will."

"How so?" Sergeant Bill LaTulipe asked. "Seriously, how?"

Lewis had an answer. It was, as a television drama once said, ripped from the headlines. "There was a shooting in Chattanooga[10] a few years ago, 2015 to be specific, inside of an Army recruiting office. Several Army personnel were killed. If you recall, in the days after the shooting, local gun owners started standing guard outside of those offices, in a well-intentioned but ill-advised attempt to provide security since military personnel who work at that office are required to be unarmed.

"The Army was none too happy about armed citizens—some of whom were associated with activist groups and militias, some associated with anti-government positions—standing vigil outside of their recruiting offices. Things could have gotten out of hand. At one point you had armed vigilantes protecting a recruiting office and local police monitoring the vigilantes. That's a situation no one wanted to see, but there it was."

Drew, Lopez, and others just shook their heads as they listened. Lewis continued.

"If all that wasn't bad enough, then in a rush to tell the story—well, tell a story—some local reporters, even some network correspondents, started doing man-on-the-street interviews with people guarding the recruiting offices, prompting concerns about copycat activities elsewhere in the country. Basically, they started making up a story to tell. Next, the Chattanooga police were being asked if they endorsed vigilante efforts to protect the United States Army."

Lopez shook his head. "That would have happened no matter what the Chattanooga police did."

"Perhaps," Lewis said, "But had the police been out front and asked citizens to *not* take on a vigilante role, then the press might—*might*—have just dismissed people standing guard as a minor sidebar. As it was, the Chattanooga police had to assign extra patrols to monitor the action of the vigilante guardsmen. Bottom line is that it is *your* responsibility to tell the story. If you don't, then someone else will. And you might not like their version of the story. This is an example of an out-of-control narrative dictating how a police department's daily operations are run."

The group was quiet, taking in what Lewis had just told them.

"One other thing. Don't create your communications—whether it is a press release or a social media post—with the idea of making the public like you. In a crisis, no one is looking to like you. They're looking for information. Period."

The session continued for another hour or so. Lewis suggested the Montgomery County police create a series of standby text messages; these would be short messages police could keep on their phones and use when communicating with incident commanders during a crisis. Lopez thought that was overkill. "How can you hold a gun as you look for an active shooter AND send a text message?" He relented to create a few generic messages, as in AM IN THE BUILDING, and INJURED CIVILIANS just to appease Lewis.

We'll never use these, LaTulipe thought, having no way to know that, one year later, he would.

One last item Lewis asked the police to consider is the establishment of so-called "reunification centers," or places where victims of mass shootings or crisis events could reunite with family members. This would involve a concerted outreach by the police to local businesses; basically, any place that had large conference rooms or waiting areas. Eventually, the police established these at the Trask Building on Udell Road and at the nearby MarLock Aerospace regional offices, also on Udell. More would be established at schools, firehouses, and other businesses that had ample parking and large open spaces indoors.

ARACAE FORD MOTORS, GAITHERSBURG, MARYLAND
CRISIS PLANNING
AUGUST 2018

Frank Aracae was late for the meeting. No matter. If the meeting or event on his schedule didn't generate revenue, then it wasn't a priority. And something that said, "Crisis Planning with Annie Lewis from LewisComm Communications" wasn't going to generate revenue, so he wasn't going to be on time. Lewis was hired to get and keep the dealership's name in the press. "Free advertising through P.R." is the way Aracae thought about it. Nothing more.

Annie Lewis had urged him to do something called crisis communication planning, but he wasn't buying her sales pitch. "We sell cars. Period. If one of those cars is in an accident, even if it was because of faulty manufacturing, well, we didn't build the car, and we sure as hell didn't drive it. So, it's somebody else's crisis," was how he thought about it.

Lewis' visit today was a part of her regular monthly in-person updates at the dealership. She had, on her own, requested a crisis communications planning session. Worse yet, from Aracae's standpoint, she asked his service and sales leads to sit in on this meeting. Aracae wasn't on board with this. So, he was going to keep the meeting extra short.

When he did step into the conference room, he saw Lewis, two sales managers, and the service bay manager.

"Welp, we sure aren't selling any cars today, are we?" Aracae said, not expecting an answer.

"Hi, Frank. Thanks for your time. Seriously," Lewis said. "I'll try to make this quick. I wanted to spend a little time talking about crisis planning for the dealership."

"And why do we need that?" Aracae said.

Lewis was ready for Aracae's shade. Or she thought she was, replying, "You may never need it and that would be fine. But there could be a fire at the dealership, cars stolen, somebody gets hurt on the premises, it could be . . ."

Aracae cut her off. "If there is a fire, the fire department talks to me. If a car is stolen or vandalized, the police talk to me. If someone gets hurt, they'll talk to my lawyer."

The silence enveloped the meeting. Everyone there, including Lewis, was used to Aracae taking up all the oxygen in the room.

"We good, then?" Aracae asked.

Everyone was silent.

"OK, meeting over. Let's go sell some cars folks. Thank you."

Everyone sat in silence.

"I mean now, people."

As the room emptied, Aracae had one "to do" on his personal list. "Annie, can you stay for a moment?"

Lewis sat back down. When the room emptied, Aracae closed the door and sat down at the conference table across from her.

"I realize doing this kind of planning is a part of what you do, and I know you do it well," Aracae said.

"Thank you," Lewis said, knowing this wasn't simply a complement.

"But this is not why I hired you."

"Mr. Aracae, I . . ."

Aracae waved a hand. "Please, it's Frank. And I hired you to get my dealership name in the newspaper. That's it."

"Frank, may I speak?"

"Sure."

"There are a lot of ways a crisis can come at a business. Many of them are completely unforeseen."

"If I can't see them, then how am I planning for them? Annie, look, I know you mean well, but this just isn't going to happen, OK?"

Lewis was silent long enough for Aracae to continue.

"I sure hope my monthly bill from LewisComm Public Relations doesn't reflect your time here today because this is not something I asked for."

"I understand, Mr. Aracae," Lewis said, looking down as she spoke.

"It's Frank. And thank you."

He walked Lewis to the door. When she slid into her car and knew she was out of earshot she muttered, "Asshole."

THE IMPLEMENTATION

Annie Lewis made it a habit to not answer her phone while driving. On this day, her phone was ringing off the hook as she drove to her office. When she arrived, she found her voicemail full. All with calls from Frank Aracae. Rather than listening to each of them she called his private cell phone number.

"Annie, thank god I reached you!"

"What's up, Frank?"

"Annie, listen, someone with Aracae Motors sold a car to the guy who drove it through the front door of the Trask building, and now a reporter wants a statement from me!"

Annie had already heard of the shooting at the Trask building, but she had not followed it in detail. She had seen tweets she crafted with the Montgomery County police. They seemed to be working well. She didn't know the angle of the story about where the car came from. Still, she needed a minute to wrap her head around what Aracae, her former client, was yammering about.

"Frank, calm down and, again, tell me what's happening."

"I'm as calm as I'm gonna get, Annie! Listen, the car that guy in Bethesda used to drive through the front door of the Trask building was purchased from us."

Lewis took a second to organize what she just heard. "OK, so someone used an Aracae Motors vehicle to commit a crime. Is that what I'm hearing?"

"Yes. We don't know what people do with the cars they buy from us. Listen, I have calls coming in from WDCN, *The Post*, and other places. They want to talk to me. Wait, hang on ..."

Lewis waited, listening to Aracae arguing about something with someone at the dealership.

"Annie! Someone from the local TV station is setting up outside!"

"Is he on your property? Because that would be trespassing."

"No, he's on the sidewalk. But his cameras are pointed right at us and ... Jesus Christ, he just started a live shot. We're on TV!!" He could see the live shot on one of the television sets in the customer waiting area.

Lewis finished taking in what Aracae was saying. She took a deep breath and replied, "And ..."

"What do you mean, 'and?' That pit bull reporter Coke Stewart is outside of my building doing a live shot saying we sold a car to a killer!" Aracae was becoming more agitated by the second.

What I have here is a rare opportunity, Lewis thought.

"Frank, what Coke Stewart is doing is what any reporter would do. He's telling the story regardless of whether Aracae Motors is a part of it."

"You need to do something, Annie! Now!!"

One more deep breath.

"Frank, do you remember a year ago when I tried to conduct a crisis communications planning session?"

"Annie, not now. I need your help with the press!"

"... and do you remember you emphatically said such planning was unnecessary?"

"Annie, don't screw with me on this ..."

"You said something along the lines of you can handle the crisis situations yourself . . ."

"ANNIE!"

"And that you definitely DID NOT WANT TO PAY ME for any crisis communications planning."

"Goddamnit, I need your help, NOW! This isn't funny."

"It wasn't funny last year, either, Frank, but you seemed to enjoy the shit out of it then," Lewis knew when the opportunity to turn a knife presented itself.

"Look, I'm sorry, OK?"

Lewis tapped a few keys on her MacBook. "Frank, have you looked at Twitter this morning?"

"What? Why?"

"Great random tweet here if you follow the #BethesdaShooter hashtag," Lewis hit a few more keys to gather her thoughts and information. "Here's a good one . . ."

"What, WHAT?"

"From someone calling themselves @SnarkMaster wrote, 'Aracae Motors. Home of the Killer Kars.'"

"JESUS CHRIST!"

"It's cute because they spelled cars with a 'k,'" Lewis said. She was enjoying this. "That's clever alliteration. Wow, it has been shared about 30 times already. They even have created an #AracaeKillerKars hashtag. It's easier to share stuff on Twitter that way, Frank."

"Annie, can we stop joking around? What should I do?"

"Frank, what you SHOULD HAVE DONE is listened to me a year ago. Right now, your best bet is damage control and triage. You can't do a thing about what people say of you on social media. You might want to write a statement saying you abhor what has happened in Bethesda . . ."

"And add that we don't approve of someone using our cars this way?" Aracae interrupted.

"That's a fucking useless and self-centered statement, Frank. Name a car dealership that delights in someone using their vehicles to kill people."

"OK, OK, then what do I say??"

"Try saying you're sorry—better yet, you are very upset—about what has happened in Bethesda, and you are praying for everyone there."

"But what about the CAR?"

"Jesus Christ, Frank. You said it a minute ago. You don't know what people who buy your cars are doing with them, but do not make that the first thing you say. Try being compassionate for once."

"OK, OK. Got it. Are you gonna email something to me?"

"Excuse me?"

"You're my P.R. gal, Annie . . ."

Time for the finishing touch. "First, we parted ways—professionally—last year when you were pissed about my asking you to do crisis communications planning . . ."

"OK, that was then and . . ."

"SECOND, DO NOT INTERRUPT ME WHEN I AM TALKING," Lewis said. The phone line on Aracae's end became deadly silent.

"And third, don't EVER refer to me as your 'P.R. gal', you pig."

Aracae tried to calm himself down. "OK, I'm sorry, can we just move on?"

Lewis was expecting that. She was finished with this jerk. She was finished a year ago. "Frank, my grandfather was a dairy farmer, did you know that?"

"No. Wait, what's this about . . ."

"Gramp had a saying that I love."

"What? What saying, Annie?"

"Mister, you have shit in your nest."

Then she hung up.

POSTSCRIPT
May 2020
News Item from CISION

SILVER SPRINGS, MARYLAND—City Cars of Silver Springs, Maryland announces that it has acquired Aracae Motors of Gaithersburg. The Ford dealership located on Wisconsin Avenue in Gaithersburg will be temporarily closed for renovations and rebranding as a City Cars location.

Aracae Motors was unfortunately forever linked to the May 24, 2019 shooting at the Trask International building in Bethesda, Maryland. A Lincoln Navigator Sport Utility Vehicle purchased at Aracae Motors a week before the shooting was used by the gunman to drive through the glass doorways of the building. The incident, where three people died, would forever brand Aracae Motors as the "Killer Kar" dealership. It was a reputation that would haunt the dealership, along with the #AracaeKillerKars hashtag, and eventually damage sales beyond recovery.

TRASK OFFICES
FOOT, NEW YORK AND BETHESDA, MARYLAND
May 24, 2019 | 4:45 p.m.

The email from Ed Reisman who was in Trask's headquarters in Foot, New York, was brief. His introduction read, "Here. Perhaps you can use this statement for press inquiries." Down at the temporary offices in Bethesda, Burt Schorr and his team read the standby press message together. Donelson read it aloud.

"We feel deeply for the victims of this horrible act?" Do we HAVE to say it that way?" Steve Donelson said, groaning more than he was speaking.

"What way do you want to say it, Steve?" Schorr asked. He was used to Donelson's penchant to incessantly fidget with copy.

How much fidgeting Donelson would be allowed was a "to be determined" topic. In some cases, changing a corporate statement—even just changing one or two words—would require a review by committee and a delay in getting the message out there. In this case, there was no room for a delay. The Associated Press was working on the story *right now* and a statement from Trask was needed right now. Here's where Reisman's "edit on the fly" rule of thumb applied.

"I mean, what does 'feel deeply' even mean?" Donelson continued. "I could get X-rated really quick with that turn of a phrase."

"Let's stay out of rabbit holes, Steve," Schorr said, stopping his employee before he went too far. "How about we just change it to read:

[...] **we feel deep sorrow for the victims of this horrible act. We will fully cooperate with the police as they conduct their investigation.**

CRISIS LIFE CYCLE
STEP TEN—DEBRIEF AND EVALUATE

CONFERENCE ROOM, TEMPORARY TRASK OFFICES
BETHESDA, MARYLAND
MAY 24, 2019 | 5:00 p.m.

It was Barron's turn to answer the phone.

"Trask offices. This is Joe Barron."

"Hi, this is Stacy Woerbling with the *Washington Post*. We're looking for information on the victims."

Barron paused. "Information?"

"Yeah, something about them. Where they lived, what they did at Trask International, what their bosses and coworkers thought of them and their work."

Barron took a breath and began, "We feel deep sorrow for the victims of this horrible act. We will fully cooperate with the police as they conduct their investigation."

"Thanks, but that's not what I'm asking for," Woerbling said. "Tell me about the victims."

"That's our statement, Ms. Woerbling. Thanks for calling."

"I don't think you understand," Woerbling began.

"I understand perfectly. We are standing by our statement," Barron repeated himself.

Woerbling was silent then quickly said, "OK, fine," before hanging up.

A scant few minutes went by before Barron's phone rang again. "It's Stacy Woerbling. I just talked to my editor. You HAVE TO tell us something about the victims."

This is one of those calls, Barron thought. "No, Ms. Woerbling, I do not have to tell you."

"But we're doing a story!"

"And that is your right," Barron said. He decided to rub it in a bit. "The U.S. Constitution says that is your right."

". . . so, we need your input to write that story!"

"Trask International respectfully declines. We are respecting the right to privacy for our employees."

Now Woerbling was pissed. "You know I can just find these families on my own."

"That is your right, yes."

Again, silence from Woerbling.

"You're not going to help, are you?"

"I gave you a statement. Would you like me to read it to you again?"

"Never mind." She hung up.

Not even a civil 'goodbye,' huh?

Barron and Donelson were handling a growing tsunami of press inquiries that afternoon.

Question: "May we come into the building to film?"

Answer: "No. This is private property, and repairs are underway."

Question: "But the images of those repairs . . ."

Answer: "This is private property. Thank you for asking, but the answer is no."

Question: "What support are you offering employees?"

Answer: "We feel deep sorrow for ..."

And on and on.

This continued for several hours. Donelson and Barron decided to break up the monotony by taking on a short writing project—producing a statement the company could use with investors and the annual report.

This short introductory narrative would be written with several audiences in mind: the news media and their readers and the Trask Board of Directors, many of whom have been asking, "What the hell is going on in Bethesda?"

Barron thought out loud as he sat down to write.

"Let's take a very direct approach. Just the facts, ma'am."

"Sure," replied Donelson. He was pacing. Adult Attention Deficit Disorder (ADD) will do that to you.

Barron started writing.

Three Trask employees were killed, seven more were seriously injured, and the Trask offices at 1041 Udell Road, Bethesda, Maryland sustained substantial damage during a shooting May 24, 2019.

"All true, sure. But it needs a different tone. Something that shows the company cares," Donelson said. Barron turned back to the keyboard. He tried to think while writing, but Donelson's constant yammering and interruptions made that very difficult to do.

Trask, Inc. is working to restore operations and assist injured families at its administrative center in Bethesda, Maryland after a mass shooting yesterday, May 24, 2019.

Donelson groaned "Christ, no. It's too impersonal. We need to show some compassion towards those who died or were injured."

"The word is T-O-W-A-R-D. No 's' at the end," said Barron, as he again turned to the keyboard. *Sometimes the smart aleck needs to be put in his place.*

But Donelson wasn't finished.

"Start with a statement of compassion, but keep in mind that investors want to know that things are still in working order. The major news outlets have already reported there was a shooting at the building, that people were injured and killed before the bastard who did it was captured."

Barron again started to write, only to again be interrupted.

"Lead with compassion but make it clear that stakeholder needs continue to be addressed."

"You through?" Barron said, giving Donelson side eye.

"For now, yeah." Donelson knew his personality could be grating on people. He also didn't care.

"So, here is some corporate spin," Barron said.

Trask, Inc. maintains its commitment to employees and stakeholders. The company has paid the funeral expenses and all medical bills for employees involved in the May 24 incident at its Bethesda, Maryland administration center. The building will open for business as usual on Tuesday, May 28, 2019.

"Oh, who the fuck are we kidding? 'Open for business as usual'?? Someone will rightfully crucify us for our insensitivity. You would think you were never in the building! You were there for God's sake."

Donelson was usually careful of his critiques, never aiming them directly at any one person.

"Steve, maybe you should give it a try," Barron said.

"No. No. Let's just change 'involved in' to 'affected by.' The company will have shrinks on site when the building reopens. Trask is paying for that, too, in addition to the ungodly cost of repairing the place, so we might as well get credit for it. Also, what about customers? You can do this, Joe."

Classic management push, Barron thought. Only Donelson wasn't his manager. He again turned to the keyboard.

Trask, Inc. is committed to its employees. The company covered all expenses and medical bills for employees affected by the May 24 mass shooting at its Bethesda, Maryland administration center. While the building sustained heavy damage, workflow was not interrupted.

Barron and Donelson were making educated guesses about expenses being covered, but it made sense, based on impromptu conversations they had with their colleagues at Trask Headquarters. Donelson had other nits to pick with Barron's writing.

"Was it a mass shooting?[11] Were enough people shot to qualify? Jesus Christ, who makes these rules, anyway? And just say there was no interruption to work performed at the building," Donelson said. The "no interruption of work" was probably a stretch, but it's a bit of corporate jargon that plays well with the intended audiences.

"We're good. Now, let's send it around for flyspecking and approval."

WE'RE good? Barron thought as he saved the document and sent it off to senior management, lawyers, human resources, and Lord knows who else would want a piece of it before the world saw what Trask had to say about anything.

As he was finishing, Donelson pushed his phone under Barron's nose.

"Oxford English Dictionary, Joe. TOWARDS is acceptable."

Barron was about to match Donelson's snark when Burt Schorr interrupted them. He had turned around on Highway 50 and drove straight back to Bethesda, arriving there only after all the fireworks had taken place.

"Guys, got a minute?" He motioned for them to come into the office where he was working.

Barron and Donelson quietly followed Schorr into his office. "Take a seat, guys," Schorr said.

"This can't be good," Donelson said.

"Burt, what's up?" Barron asked.

"Corporate has decided we—the three of us—are not to be involved with any public relations activities related to what happened yesterday."

"Why?" Barron and Donelson asked in a surprise act of unison.

"We're already knee-deep in the hoopla," Donelson said.

Shorr put up his hand in a "stop it" motion. "Headquarters thinks we're too close to the situation. They say for us, it isn't business. It's personal."

"Bull," said Donelson.

"Life's a bitch, Steve. What can I say? This decision is out of our hands."

Barron became silent and started staring off into the distance.

"Guys, let me let you hear it from the horse's mouth," Schorr said, punching a number into his phone. In a moment Ed Reisman was on the line.

"Hi, guys. I'm sure Burt has informed you of our decision."

"This isn't right or fair, Ed," Donelson started. "It's the biggest story of the year at Trask and ..."

"Stop. Right there, Steve," Reisman said. That was very unlike Reisman, who was big on letting everyone have their say. "This is not a fly-by-the-seat-of-your-pants decision. If a Coke Stewart or some other reporter gets wind of the fact that the Trask spokesperson they are talking to was in the building when Tomlinson went on his shooting spree, then the story takes on a new dimension, a life of its own. That would not be productive."

Barron and Donelson were silent.

"We need the focus to be on how we are getting back to business as usual," Reisman said. "Look, you don't have to agree with me on this, but the decision has been made."

Donelson decided to play a different hand. "So, what if I were to call Coke Stewart and say I was in the building? Are you saying I can't do that?"

Reisman was ready for this. "Steve, you are free to talk to any reporter about any subject you like. You already know this, but in that situation, you are not talking on behalf of Trask, Inc. You are representing yourself."

Donelson knew his second-line supervisor was right. He didn't have to say anything.

"Besides, Steve. This is not the biggest story as far as Trask is concerned. It's a human tragedy that we are dealing with. And you already know that."

Barron remained still.

"Joe, you OK? I haven't heard a peep out of you," Reisman said.

"No, I'm OK, Ed. Just disappointed. That's all."

"Nobody wants to be dealing with this right now," Reisman said. "There are going to be more than a few uncomfortable conversations that will take place between Trask International and the press in the coming days."

Donelson spoke up again. A thin slice of defiance remained in his voice. "So, who is going to take the lead on press inquiries?"

"Geeta Allen up here in Westchester County. She was fielding questions when Tomlinson was on his joy ride through the building, and she has done a good job."

Barron smiled and nodded his head. Donelson saw that motion and muttered, "You would be happy."

"Excuse me?" Schorr heard that and was not going to let it pass.

"Nothing," Donelson said.

Reisman cleared his throat. "OK, I have the statement Steve and Joe prepared. We'll review that up here and have it ready for use. Guys, thank you for your dedication. I am even more thankful you are OK. Most people would have just stayed home rather than jump back into the fray. And no one would blame them for that. Burt, thanks for bringing me into the conversation."

Schorr ended the call. Donelson and Barron got up to leave.

"Steve, stick around, will ya?"

Donelson sat back down as Barron left the office. Schorr spoke up as soon as the door closed.

"Is there some issue between you and Geeta Allen?"

"Nope."

"Then enlighten me as to why you said what you did to Joe."

"It was inappropriate of me to say that. Joe and Geeta may have a thing going on ..."

"Which is perfectly OK if they do, right?" Schorr was not going to let THAT kind of opinion get into the mix.

"You're absolutely right. I was wrong, Burt. Just frustrated that I won't be a part of the press outreach."

Schorr took a deep breath before continuing. "I don't have to tell you that's a dangerous and slippery slope you stepped out on just then."

"I know, I know. Geeta is a solid professional, and she was not given the assignment just because of who she is or what she was doing yesterday."

"That's right. Look, I don't think Joe was offended, and I doubt Ed heard anything. Just watch yourself. You won't like where that attitude will take you."

"Understood. Should I apologize to Joe?"

"That might be a good idea, yes."

Donelson left and walked straight over to Barron. "Hey buddy, got a second?"

Barron looked at Donelson. "You're forgiven."

"What?"

"I said you're forgiven. You're a classic Type A personality with no 'mute' button. I get it. You're forgiven."

"Thanks, I . . ."

"You're also an asshole. Now, let's get back to work."

Donelson nodded his head. "Yep, let's get back to work."

TRASK INTERNATIONAL BUILDING
BETHESDA, MARYLAND
MAY 24, 2019 | 6:38 p.m.

Outside of the Trask building, Captain Kelly Mayer was talking to Rupert Levitt, the site manager for the Udell Road building.

"OK, Mr. Levitt, detectives are finished with the crime scene. The building is yours."

"Thanks, Captain Mayer."

Mayer looked at the building before speaking. "You have quite a mess in there, I'm afraid. May take you a while to clean it up."

"We're up to the task. Thanks," Levitt said. *Lady, you have no idea what's about to happen here.*

Mayer walked off as Levitt punched a number in on his phone. Alexis Shimada answered as Levitt said, "Alexis, we have the building back . . ."

"Thanks, Rupert. Call in the calvary. CEO wants the building looking like nothing happened by Tuesday morning."

"That's a big task, Alexis."

"You're going to tell me it'll cost a fortune, and I'll tell you the boss doesn't care."

"OK, understood," Levitt said. He ended the call and thought, *It's going to cost several fortunes. But it ain't my money, and someone else up north still will bitch about it.*

TRASK HEADQUARTERS
MAY 25, 2019
7:10 a.m.

"You understand that we are charging triple overtime, don't you, Ms. Shimada?" The question was coming from a drywall contractor, one of five Trask International hired to repair the walls in the Udell Road building before Tuesday morning, May 28.

"I get it, yes. It's important that the work be done on time. YOU understand that we expect you to be finished by end-of-day on Monday, May 27, correct?" Shimada responded.

"Can do. We are getting extra personnel in to do the work." The contractor was silent for a second before adding, "I'm sorry we have to meet under these circumstances."

"Me, too. And it's OK. It isn't your fault or mine," Shimada said. She finished the call, then looked at her messages. One was from Rupert Levitt in Bethesda. She called Levitt immediately.

"Alexis, hello. Listen, we can't source glass doors to repair the south foyer of the building. At least we cannot source something by Tuesday morning."

This was a biggie on the "fix the building to-do" list. The entrance must look like nothing happened. As is, someone had driven a big SUV through the door and that was one ugly looking problem that needed fixing. Shimada let out an audible sigh.

"So, we're screwed. Is that where we are?" Shimada said.

"Not exactly. I have an idea but knowing you are insistent on a 'back to normal' look, I wanted to run it by you first," Levitt said.

"Shoot," Shimada replied, immediately regretting her choice of words.

Levitt explained that the foyers at the north and south ends of the building comprise two sets of 15-foot-high double glass doors. There was a small breezeway between the two doorways. Levitt said workers could remove one set of doors from the north end of the building and insert them at the south entrance. "It'll look close to normal, Alexis. Close enough that most people may not even notice."

"You're absolutely sure we can't get new doors by Monday?" It was one of those questions Shimada knew could rankle Levitt, but she had to ask it. It may have been Memorial Day weekend, but Shimada was on a mission that needed to be finished.

"If I drove to the factory myself and offered to strap the new doors on the roof of my Hyundai, I still couldn't get it done in time, Alexis. It's just a matter of sourcing the materials. Those doors were special orders when the building was built. They still are."

"OK, let's go with your suggestion." Shimada said. "And Rupert..."

"Yeah?"

"Thank you. You are doing amazing work down there."

"Thank you, Alexis. These are trying times."

"Did you have to change your Memorial Day weekend plans for this?"

"Yep. Wife and kids are in Ocean City."

"We're going to make it up to you. I promise."

"You bet your ass you are," Levitt said while chuckling.

The procedure Levitt designed to move one set of doors was no simple undertaking. They were too heavy to just get a crew of six to eight men and carry them from one end of the building to the other. Instead, a forklift and a front loader had to be brought in. Both pieces of equipment were wheeled close enough to the outer door at the entrance of the building. Then one crew would line the bed of the front loader with enough blankets and safety pads while another work crew straps lift belts to the outer door and uses the forklift to, once freed of their hinges, lift the door out of position and gently place it in the loading bed of the front loader. A four-person crew then escorted the front loader as it slowly drove to the opposite side of the building to place the door in its new, temporary home. One nasty bump on the trip could result in the glass door snapping in two, then really putting the "back to normal" plans in a state of array ... or "all over the floor," which was the term Trask International used when plans fell apart.

That same procedure needed to be repeated in order to move the inner door 15 feet forward to its new, temporary location.

One other substantial expense involved the carpeting. There was blood in multiple places, including upstairs where Tom Larry died, downstairs at the reception desk where Carl Wilson took his last breath, and 30 feet away where Carla Augustine was shot in the head.

Levy identified two options for the carpeting: cut the blood-stained portion of the carpet out and replace that only, or replace the carpet in the entire 3,500-square-foot lobby. The answer came quickly enough when Levy realized it would be impossible to match the carpeting in the lobby. New carpeting was then ordered for the full lobby and the upstairs hallway. There were enough breaks in the floor to simply replace the carpeting where Larry died. The color was kept close enough to what was there in hopes that no one would notice.

Item last on the repair agenda was one piece of construction that would leave the exterior of the building looking very different. Four concrete bollards, each painted bright yellow, were installed at the base of the concrete walkway leading up to the building doorways. Their purpose was abundantly clear: keep someone from driving a car up the sidewalk and through the door.

When someone asked Shimada if the installation of the bollards was an extreme step, rationalizing that employees would feel safe enough without the bollards serving as a reminder, Shimada's answer was simple and straightforward, "You could install a set of fifty caliber machine guns at each door and I doubt people would ever feel as safe as they did before May 24." The answer was unsatisfying to the naysayers, but the arguments petered out after hearing her response.

Shimada remained a one-person whirlwind of activity. She asked Mary Doane to work up a spreadsheet showing the possible costs of an emergency room visit for each and every person who worked at the Udell Road building. An independent think tank, Consumer Health Ratings[12], estimates that the average cost of a visit to an emergency room, providing that said visit is only for a single outpatient procedure, is about $1,200. Shimada seemed to recall similar numbers from the National Institutes of Health. Those numbers seemed surprisingly steady, considering that the Consumer Health Ratings research was from 2013. Still, it was a good enough number to go with.

Also, not everyone in the Udell Road building went to a hospital, so not everyone will run up a hospital bill.

"Math is pretty simple here," Shimada said to herself. "Twelve hundred dollars times 130 persons is just under $140,000. Round it up to $200K." She contemplated that number for a few minutes, then called Ed Reisman and Ron Reynolds.

"Guys, we should cover any out-of-pocket expenses employees have for medical insurance for the next two weeks."

"What? Why?" Reisman asked.

"Let's call it good corporate citizenship. People in that building have been through the ringer in the last 24 hours. Let's not make their lives any more complicated by filling out insurance paperwork. If anyone had to go to the hospital because of yesterday's incident, then they can just send us the bill, and we'll pay it. It's a damn sight better than defending ourselves in a negligence lawsuit."

"It is potentially fuel for someone to use against us in just such a lawsuit, too," Reynolds said. He knew his training was to look for the legal boogeymen at every corner. Still, Shimada's recommendation made sense.

"Is this something we want to tell the world about?" Reisman said, already knowing the answer.

"No, not at all," Shimada said. "We want to keep this on the down low. If word gets out, then fine. We admit this is something we're doing because we believe in ..."

"... care for the individual," Reynolds finished her sentence.

Oh, look, the old dog is learning a new trick, Shimada thought.

"OK," Reisman said. "This is something for us to have as a potential Q&A. We mark it carefully, so it is used ONLY if we are asked about it by a reporter."

"Why two weeks, Alexis?" Reynolds asked.

"Someone may wait a few days before going to the hospital. We're giving everyone a very generous grace period. After two weeks, then it is back to filling out insurance reimbursement forms. My team worked as hard on those as they have on this idea."

Shimada had two more items on her to-do list. One was to find local psychiatric counselors who could be on call at the building come Tuesday morning. Anyone feeling stressed about being back at work can visit the counselor for free. She found two, each charging $5,000 for one week's worth of their time. She also secured an agreement from the Montgomery County District Attorney's office to have someone from that office present a regular update on Tomlinson's trial. "I don't care if they're talking to an empty room. It's important we show employees that we're being completely transparent," she said.

Last Item. Anyone who did not feel safe coming back to work shouldn't have to. Trask was not yet on board with a work from home arrangement, but these were unusual circumstances.

TRASK OFFICES IN BETHESDA
SATURDAY, MAY 25, 2019 | 11 a.m.

Joe Barron punched in the number for Daniel Lucille, the supervisor for Carla Augustine, the woman who Tomlinson killed with a single shot to the head. He had written a death notice for the *Washington Post* which Trask would pay for, but it had to be approved by Augustine's family. He set up a conference call between Lucille and Augustine's husband, Anthony. Lucille was going to slowly read the death notice to Anthony and get his verbal approval to use it.

"Now, Tony, I have to stress that you don't have to do this," Lucille said.

Barron felt himself squirm. Reisman's crew wanted this death notice published. Trask was doing virtually no outreach with respect to the repairs to the building, the presence of counselors, and the work from home option, so it seemed like the death notices for Augustine, Frank Lary, and Wilson are the only visible things Trask was doing. With being taken off the media relations aspect of the company response, these death notices also represented the only tangible evidence that Barron did anything in the days following the shooting.

It took Lucille almost five minutes to read a 700-word death notice, but in the end Anthony Augustine approved the notice without any changes. Not that any changes would have mattered; Trask International was mentioned only once in the death notice, so it wasn't as though Trask was getting P.R. miles out of doing this. He no sooner finished that thought when he started hating himself for thinking it.

Steve Donelson had his to-do as well, and he was none too happy about it. Trask wanted to let employees know that the company would make only a brief comment about the shooting.

No other public statements would be made. It was a personal tragedy for those involved, and the executives at headquarters felt that less was more. Simply say the company felt sorrow for the loss of lives—basically a version of the statement Ed Reismann wrote—and that's it.

However, employees should know that they could talk to the press if they wanted. Just because Trask International was not talking to the press did not mean no one could. Trask International took the position that this is a free country, and if someone wanted to talk to a reporter about what happened on May 24—even if they wanted to throw Trask under the proverbial bus because of what happened—then fine. It is an individual choice.

This is because I bitched to Reisman about not doing the press anymore? Donelson thought. He put a halfhearted effort into writing an internal message to employees, which read, in part, "Trask is not going to engage in lengthy interviews with the press about the events that transpired on May 24. Any employee who wishes to talk to the press may do so on their own."

His writing was clumsy. Donelson didn't see the conflict with saying there would be a shrink on site or that people could work from home (*Not work is more like it*, Donelson thought) if they felt unsafe returning to the office right away and go ahead and talk to the press if they wanted.

And no one looked too closely at the message Donelson wrote. Until of course, Donelson and H.R. were accused of threatening employees should they talk to the press about the shooting.

"Are you saying my job is on the line, should I speak to the press?" one anonymous writer said via the company's internal "complaint box" system, called What's on Your Mind?

"Typical big company move," was another.

It took no time at all before the misunderstood message was shared on social media.

@StandUpSam
Typical big business snuffing out the voice of freedom.

@SallyBee
Maybe they'll like having their words thrown back at them?

@HarryLu
Hey @TraskIntl, you ever gonna learn?

It took an additional effort by Geeta Allen to compose a tweet:

@TraskIntl
Hey, guys, we're sorry. Clumsy message there. Just meant anyone who wants to talk to the press—no matter what they want to say . . . good or bad—is free to go ahead. Apologize for the misunderstanding . . . that was all on us.

The "hate tweets" died down after a few hours. Donelson was going to take the "clumsy message" passage as an affront, but his conversation with Schorr made him decide to hold his tongue.

RADIO STATION WAMU
WASHINGTON, D.C.
JUNE 5, 2019

INTERVIEW HOST RANDALL COOPER: "Well, that concludes our interview with Lorraine DellaBoniva and Gus Henlopen, board members for Trask International, and members of diametric opposite organizations when it comes to the topic of guns. Ms. DellaBoniva is a member of Parents Demand Action, and Mr. Henlopen is a longtime American Handgun Association member. That puts my guests on the polar opposite ends of the gun control spectrum."

Henlopen: "I wouldn't say we are on opposite ends of a spectrum, Randall. Lorraine and I both feel strongly, and the same way, about what happened in Bethesda."

DellaBoniva: "Agreed. That individual should never have been armed."

Henlopen: "We have said for years there is a mental health crisis in the country and . . ."

DellaBoniva (Laughing): "Let's stop there, Gus, and remain on the same side of the issue."

Henlopen (Laughing): "I agree. Thank you."

Cooper: "Thank you both. I appreciate your time."

Cooper shut down the phone lines, and Henlopen waited a moment before calling DellaBoniva directly.

"Lorraine, I hung around to thank you. We have different opinions about guns, but we both discussed the issue with intelligence and maturity."

"Thank YOU, Gus. So did you. That's the only way we make progress as a society."

Henlopen was quiet for a moment, then spoke. "Did you buy that handgun I recommended?"

"I did. A Glock G19, 9 mm. Thank you for the recommendation."

"You're welcome."

"And thank you, Gus, for not bringing that up during the interview."

"It wasn't germane to the topic. Have a good afternoon, Lorraine."

"You, too, Gus."

THE AFTERMATH
Rinse and Repeat

BERWYN, PENNSYLVANIA**
June 7, 2019

** This event, while all fiction as explained here, is based on a true incident that happened in April 2021 in Pennsylvania.

It was senior prom season in Berwyn, Pennsylvania, a suburb of Philadelphia, and seniors from Prairie Schooner High School were at a local restaurant celebrating.

"Pre-gaming" is how they call it. Party before the party. Couples were decked out in cocktail dresses and tuxedos. That included Simon Bellows and his boyfriend, Leonard. Bellows had long ago come out to his family and friends as gay. This evening, he was going to celebrate who he was. Leonard was wearing a sharp black tuxedo, and Bellows had on a full-length dress. His makeup and jewelry—earrings, necklaces, bracelets—were a perfect match. Bellows and Leonard were among eight students, four couples, seated at a table at the General von Steuben Inn. They were laughing and enjoying each other's company.

Perhaps a bit loud. Whether they were too loud was open for debate. But Carl Ransome thought they were too loud. He was trying to enjoy dinner with his wife and another couple at a nearby table when the noise from the Prairie Schooner table became too much. He arose and swiftly walked over to the Prairie Schooner table, stopping right behind Bellows, who he didn't at first realize was a man.

"Will you kids just keep it down!" he shouted.

"Will you just mind your own damn business," Bellows said as he turned around.

Ransome stepped back in a moment of shock. "Holy shit! You're a dude!"

"Nothing gets past you, does it?" Bellows said.

"YOU LOOK RIDICULOUS!" Ransome said. People at other tables were starting to look in their direction.

Caroline Locker, one of the teens at the table, pulled out her phone and immediately started recording, pointing the camera directly at Ransome.

"Just leave us alone!" Bellows shouted at Ransome.

"Who dresses you?" Ransome said.

"Carl, please just come back here and sit down," his wife said. Locker made sure she caught Mrs. Ransome on camera, too. Especially the part where Mr. Ransome jerked his arm away from his wife when she tried pulling him away from Bellows.

Ransome wasn't moving. He just stood before Bellows and smirked. "Wear a suit like a man."

"Just leave us the fuck alone!!" Bellows shouted.

By this time several other people had their phones out. Several were doing live videos on Facebook.

The maître d' from the General von Steuben Inn arrived. "Please, if you cannot keep your voices down, then I will have to ask everyone to leave."

Ransome felt he'd had his say. He gave Bellows a smug look and walked back to his table.

But the damage was done. Bellows sat down, put his head on Leonard's shoulder. A tear rolled down his cheek. "It's OK. He's just an asshole," Leonard said softly.

Ransome left, feeling like he had enjoyed his pound of flesh. He was used to reading people the riot act. He was a regional sales executive for Trask International, so chewing out a sales professional was second nature to him. *No big deal*, he thought.

He thought wrong. A video of him berating a young man over his sexuality was going viral. And his photo and name were making their way through Twitter.

> @TheYoungAngrys
> **Homophobic POS harasses kid on his prom night for wearing a dress.**

The tweet was complete with a picture of a smirking Ransome.

> @RighetousMom44017
> **Who is this guy???**

> @MAHTceo
> **Someone has to identify this jerk and have his employer fire him!**

This tweet included a screen capture of Ransome standing toe to toe with Bellows.

> @TheYoungAngrys
> **Got it. He's Carl Ransome and he works for @TraskIntl. Jerk.**

> @RighetousMom44017
> Hey, @TraskHumanResources, when are you gonna fire this guy?

Those first five tweets were shared, liked, and repeated by others and joined by more tweeters nearly 1,000 times in less than an hour. Carl Ransome, who himself had no Twitter account, was trending. He wouldn't know it, since that morning he was sleeping off the two bottles of wine he polished off while dining at the General von Steuben Inn.

Alexis Shimada was also asleep at her house. Her phone started buzzing before 6 a.m. Messages from Mary Doane and an attorney in Ron Reynolds' office. "You need to look at your Twitter account. Stat," Doane said.

A few thumb swipes on her phone and Shimada was already slapping her forehead. "Jesus Christ. Carl Ransome!? No."

Two minutes later Ed Reisman was on the phone with Shimada. "What the hell is a Carl Ransome?" he said. From Reisman's planning materials, this looked like a Level 4 Crisis. It was not going to disrupt the day-to-day flow of business, but it was going to give Trask a black eye.

"He's a regional sales executive for the Mid-Atlantic Region."

"OK, are you sure he works for us?"

"Positive."

"Why so positive?"

"Ed, Carl Ransome was Mel Tomlinson's second-line supervisor."

Reisman was quiet for a moment. He knew who Mel Tomlinson was, but his internal synapses were momentarily misfiring. He finally spoke. "OK, how well-known is that? I mean, would someone on Twitter or with a news outlet make that connection?"

"Probably not, Ed. But there are plenty of people inside of Trask who know who Tomlinson worked for, and . . ."

JOE DIORIO | 185

"... and they're all on Twitter," Reisman finished Shimada's thought for her.

"Someone at the restaurant knows Ransome well enough to tell the world he works for us. Not only that, that same person or someone close to them probably knows Trask well enough to say Ransome's actions certainly don't represent 'care for the individual.' Heck, I can probably set my watch to that one."

Reisman chuckled, "Is this like saying someone on *Star Trek* disobeyed the Prime Directive?" He was referring to the rule that exists in the fictional show and movies dictating that interference with another society is strictly forbidden. In this case, Trask's long-standing H.R. mantra is well-known to the public.

"Yeah, pretty much," Shimada answered. There was no hesitation in her voice.

"I figure you have been in touch with Ron Reynolds?"

"Someone from his office alerted me to this, so yeah."

Considering that Ransome had a dotted line to Mel Tomlinson elevated this to a Level 3 Crisis, bad enough to temporarily disrupt daily operations. Reynolds was soon on a conference call with Shimada, Reisman, and Sylvester "Sly" Moore, the senior vice president of marketing for Trask and Ransome's boss.

"Fire his ass. Period," Moore said. He wanted no part of Ransome, even though his demeanor suggest he and Ransome come from a similar school of people management.

"Let's not look so knee-jerk like," Reisman said. "Can we suspend him from his responsibilities and say it is pending further investigation? We don't want to look like we are bending to public opinion."

"Even though we are," Moore said.

"No, we're not," Shimada responded as quickly as she could. "This guy is being a jerk and a homophobe. His stupid actions are out there for every customer to see if they choose to take two minutes and look him up on the internet. Yes, he should be fired if what's being shown on those videos is true …" Shimada knew she should be careful not to refer to Ransome as a jerk, but time was working against this team, and the crisis level was slowly escalating.

"And that's the key point," Reynolds said. "We should take the time to speak to him and—this is the part you're going to hate—find an eyewitness or two and ask them about it."

"We know his wife was there. Can she testify against him?" Moore asked.

"This isn't a court of law, so yes. If she agrees to, that is. We would be taking away her livelihood, too. Regardless, we should have someone else."

"Simon Bellows should be easy enough to find," Reisman said.

"Plenty easy," Reynolds said. "He's on *Good Morning America* right now."

That was quick, Reisman thought. "So, we know his name, and we know the name of the high school he attends. Ron, can someone from your office reach out to the high school to contact him?"

"Should it be someone from legal?"

"Given the circumstances, it's the least of all evils," Reisman said. "If I or someone in corporate communications reaches out, then word could get out that the Trask P.R. folks are in contact with Simon Bellows, and the message gets twisted into Trask trying to create a positive P.R. spin."

"And if I contact them, the assumption will automatically be made that Ransome is about to be fired," Shimada said.

Reynolds thought it over, then said, "OK, we can do it. I can frame it as fact finding, which it is of course."

"We need an immediate response on social media," Reisman said. "Is it accurate to say that Ransome will be relieved of his duties immediately pending an investigation?"

"We need to tell HIM that first," Shimada said.

"I have him on my speed dial," Moore said. "Please give me the pleasure of calling him to ruin his day."

"Sylvester, stop it right there," Reynolds said; he was practically shouting, but he wanted his point across. "Look, if Ransome really did this—and from what we see on social media it sure as heck looks like he did—then we need to be one thousand percent sure we are giving him every drop of due diligence and then some."

Reynolds continued, "Yes, you contact him and say that based on the initial reports, you are going to suspend his work activities. He's still on the payroll. Right now, we are just paying him to cool his jets, got it?"

Moore was silent.

"GOT IT?" Reynolds said. This time he was shouting.

"Got it, Ron. No need to yell."

"If you think the situation is fucked up now, just go ahead and let your primal instincts guide you."

"Ron, do you want to call him with me?" Moore said.

Reynolds let that suggestion marinate for a second, then said, "Yes. You do the talking, but if I have to butt in, then you and I are going to have an unpleasant conversation afterwards."

Moore and Reynolds logged off the call. Reisman and Shimada agreed that Reisman would write a tweet for Shimada to review—Reynolds will need to see it, too, but they were confident he understood the need for speed in this situation.

The moment he was off the call, Reisman started writing:

"Trask is aware of the unfortunate situation involving one of our employees that occurred at the General von Steuben Inn. We have temporarily relieved this employee of his day-to-day responsibilities pending a review of the facts."

He hit "send" so it went to Shimada and Reynolds.

Reynolds responded first, "Take out the word 'unfortunate.'

It is unfortunate, but I don't want to give any hater a chance to jump on us. Even over how we may categorize something."

"Thanks," Reisman said. "How'd the call go with Ransome?"

"About as smoothly as expected." He didn't need to say anything else.

Geeta Allen was looped in and immediately sent out the following tweet:

> @TraskIntl
> **Trask is aware of the unfortunate situation involving one of our employees that occurred at the General von Steuben Inn. We have temporarily relieved this employee of his day-to-day responsibilities pending a review of the facts.**

Ron Reynolds was on Reisman in a nanosecond.

"Ed, I said REMOVE the word 'unfortunate'! Jesus."

Reisman looked at the tweet and knew instantly the fault was his. "I'm sorry, Ron. That was my mistake. I sent it to Geeta immediately and neglected to include your edit."

"Well, we won't be bored this morning," Reynolds said. "Someone on my team has already spoken to Simon Bellows, and he confirmed it was Ransome who verbally accosted him."

Shimada was looped in again.

"We need to keep moving on this," Reisman said. "Alexis, who is Ransome's number two?"

"Kelly Prior. She's talented."

"She now has Ransome's job. Let me write the next tweet."

"You sure, Ed?" Reynolds wasn't being sarcastic, he saw the tweets:

> @CAPT_SNARK
> **Hey, @TraskIntl. I guess this is unfortunate. Just like how you are protecting this shitbag.**

The tweet had 200 likes in seconds. "Sometimes you have to take it on the chin," Reisman said.

In yet another impromptu conference call, Shimada, Reynolds, and Reisman confirmed that Ransome would be fired. He would get 60-days pay and remain on company benefits during that time. He also would receive any pending sales commissions due to him.

If the haters disliked the first tweet, then they're gonna despise this one, Reisman thought as he wrote. He did it with Shimada and Reynolds on a conference call. When Geeta Allen hit "send," the following message appeared.

> **@Trask Intl**
> **After careful consideration, Trask International has terminated its employment with Carl Ransome, effective immediately. Kelly Prior now is the acting Vice President of Sales, effective immediately.**

A contingency Q&A set was prepared and put into action almost immediately.

"Geeta, hi. It's Coke Stewart from WJKA in Washington, D.C. Is it true that Carl Ransome was Mel Tomlinson's supervisor?"

Allen was ready for that one. "Our sales organization constantly undergoes reorganizations, Coke. I don't have that information immediately available."

"OK, but is this something you can find out?"

"As long as it isn't violating employee privacy rules, sure."

Momentary pause.

"Is Carl Ransome completely off your payroll?"

"He is no longer employed by Trask International, Inc."

"But is he getting a buyout?"

"No." *That* was true. Ransome was simply receiving 60-days' notice of termination, in line with state and federal employment laws. Stewart had just asked the wrong question, and it wasn't Allen's job to correct him.

"OK, last question for now ... did Trask put a woman in place of Carl Ransome to reduce criticism?"

"Kelly Prior was promoted because she is the best person qualified within Trask for the job."

"Were other candidates considered?"

"We always evaluate talent, Coke." That was a freelance response, but one she was comfortable with.

"Can I talk to her?"

"I can ask if she's available, OK?"

"Can you do it by my deadline?"

"No promises there." She sent an email to Prior, confident that she would not get a response right away. The step of sending the email would give Allen a clear mind should Stewart ask again.

The remainder of that Saturday and Sunday were relatively quiet. There was some buzz on Twitter about the situation, but Trask International was reaping the benefits of making a sound decision in a timely fashion. Allen didn't bother making Stewart's request to interview Kelly Prior a priority, and there was no follow up from him on that subject.

Then Monday morning arrived. Allen's phone was buzzing even as she parked her car in the parking lot of Trask International's Foot, New York, headquarters.

She could see it was Coke Stewart calling. *Probably going to bitch that I didn't get him and Kelly Prior connected.* She put that thought aside and answered. "Hey, Coke. Happy Monday."

"Hi Geeta. Hey, I have a follow up for you regarding the Carl Ransome story ..."

"Yeah, Coke. I'm sorry, but I haven't heard back from Kelly Prior yet and ..."

"It isn't that. Geeta, I learned that Carl Ransome was Mel Tomlinson's supervisor. We're going with that story today."

JOE DIORIO | 191

Allen was somewhat stunned.

"OK."

"Is there anything Trask wants to say?"

Don't lie, but don't answer right now.

"Coke, I need to confirm a few things before responding."

"Nothing to confirm, Geeta. I already know Ransome managed Tomlinson and was the one who fired him. This is a good story about someone getting their comeuppance, don't you think?"

"Let me confirm a few things before responding. When is your deadline?"

"I can hold the story for thirty minutes, Geeta."

"Gimme an hour."

"Forty-five minutes, tops."

"Deal." She ended the call and immediately moved to call Ed Reisman.

"I'm right behind you, Geeta," Reisman said. He was walking from the parking lot, too.

Allen turned to her second line manager and briefed him on what she just learned. Reisman immediately called Alexis Shimada, who was already in her office. Five minutes later, the three of them were in Shimada's office with Ron Reynolds on a conference call.

"Alexis, what were the circumstances of Tomlinson's firing?" Reisman asked.

"Separation, Ed. We don't say fired," Reynolds said.

"Ron, that dog won't hunt with the press. Tomlinson was let go. Call it what you want, but now a Washington, D.C. ABC affiliate knows that Tomlinson's manager was fired."

"Before we get too far down the rabbit hole, here are some facts," Shimada said. "We NEVER released this information, but Tomlinson was on his second improvement plan when we finally let him go."

"OK, what's an improvement plan?" Allen asked.

"You're a good employee, so you wouldn't know," Reisman said, giving Allen a friendly elbow nudge.

"We do those when someone isn't meeting their job expectations. Tomlinson was put on an improvement plan in 2015 and again late in 2016. He had to attend some training classes and overall improve his sales results. It isn't pretty when we are working with sales and marketing professionals."

"How so?"

"This isn't *Glengarry Glen Ross*. Everyone has sales figures they need to meet, but we do understand when the leads are weak," Shimada said.

"But Tomlinson was eventually told to hit the bricks," Reisman said. "OK, the intent behind my original question is this: was it just Carl Ransome alone in the room with Tomlinson when he was fired … OK, separated?"

"No, of course not. There was a representative from human resources there to answer any questions. Also, Sylvester Moore was there, too. He may have been on speaker phone, but this definitely wasn't a one-on-one conversation."

Mary Doane came into the office with a folder. "Here is Tomlinson's separation letter."

Shimada pulled out the letter and quickly scanned it. "Here is something you can work with, Ed. At the bottom of this letter is Sylvester Moore's signature and Mel Tomlinson's signature."

"So, there is no paper trail that connects Tomlinson to Ransome," Allen said.

"I'm afraid that may be little more than splitting hairs," Reynolds said. "Ransome was in Tomlinson's line of command."

"Guys, the important part of this is that the letter says, 'we agree to a separation.' Separation, not firing. And Tomlinson signed it."

"You're not suggesting I show this to the press?"

"No, but we can say his departure was a mutual agreement."

"Can we also say there were near Herculean efforts made to keep Tomlinson as a Trask International employee?" Reisman was looking for the most positive spin he could think of.

"What if we say Tomlinson's SEPARATION from Trask International came about after extensive efforts to train and prepare him for a successful career, but the decision was mutual that we part ways?" Allen asked.

"Let me see that in writing, Geeta," Reynolds said. "I think you are on the right track."

"What if we are a bit more compassionate?" Reisman said.

The statement was finished, and Allen forwarded it on to the press.

STATEMENT FROM TRASK INTERNATIONAL FOR WJKA VIA COKE STEWART

Per your request, Melvin Tomlinson is a former employee of Trask International, Inc. He worked in sales and consulting during his time with the company. Tomlinson and Trask International agreed to bring his employment to an end in 2017. This came after several years of personally working with Tomlinson to ensure he would have a successful Trask International career.

Stewart read the statement, then asked, "But Carl Ransome was his supervisor, right?"

"Carl Ransome was Tomlinson's first line manager, yes."

"And he fired Tomlinson, right?"

"It was not a one-person decision. His separation from Trask International came about after a lengthy period of time."

"So, he was a bad employee?"

"Coke, that is a subject area we will not discuss."

"What about Ransome? Was he a lousy supervisor?"

"We don't discuss individual employee situations."

"Ransome isn't a Trask International employee anymore."

"We are sticking by our statement. We have said in the past, and we will continue to maintain this position, that we do not discuss individual employee situations."

"Geeta, you just confirmed that Mel Tomlinson was fired. That's an individual employee."

"I never said he was fired. And I am only providing confirmation of something you and I know you already know."

Stewart was silent for a moment.

"It's been 40 minutes since we talked. When are you running your story?" Allen had a reason she was asking.

"Next few minutes, Geeta."

"OK. We done?"

"I think so. Thanks."

"Thank you, Coke."

TWEET FROM @WJKA

> Just learned that the former @TraskIntl employee fired for a homophobic rant was the former supervisor of the #BethesdaShooting perp. Details at our website.

STORY POSTED ONLINE ON THE WJKA WEBSITE

JUNE 22, 2019—WJKA has learned that Carl Ransome, the Trask International employee who was fired last week after a video of him engaging in a homophobic rant, was the supervisor of Melvin Tomlinson, the former Trask International employee who just last month engaged in a violent and bloody mass shooting at Trask's Bethesda, Maryland offices.

Ransome was part of the Trask International management team involved in the ultimate decision to let Tomlinson go in 2017. Trask did not give a reason for Tomlinson's dismissal, saying only that it came about after lengthy efforts to keep him on the payroll.

Allen had all of her social media monitoring tools working overtime.

> @Young Angrys
> **Serves @TraskIntl right**

> @HRguy
> **What training did this guy get? Firearms?**

> @Justice4Bethesda
> **Never would have happened with good gun control**

> @NRA4Evah
> **Oh, will you PUL-EEZE stop . . .**

"Chatter on Twitter is going as expected, I suppose," Reisman said.

"Yeah. There was no easy path on this one."

"Hey, we told the truth, and we didn't burn any bridges or damage any reputations," Reisman said. "Good job, Geeta."

Allen turned back to her desk but noticed someone else standing nearby. It was Joe Barron.

"Hey stranger," Allen said.

"Hey. Anybody hungry? It's almost lunchtime."

"Definitely."

"Was that answer in your contingency Q&A?"

Allen looked down at her desk, smiled, then said, "Nope. Let's get out of here."

NEXT UP
(And There's Always A Next Up)

Reisman did a phone conference for a quick debriefing on the Bethesda shooting. Shimada, Reisman, Dekker, and Moore were on the call.

"From a communications standpoint, things went about as well as could be expected," Reisman said. "There was no shortage of news stories about the incident, but none were blaming us."

"Not even Coke Stewart's coverage," Reynolds said. He wasn't happy that personnel stories at Trask International became a part of the story, but there was no substantial damage to daily business operations and, as of right now, no one was filing a lawsuit against Trask International accusing the company of helping this tragedy happen.

"This was probably the worst crisis we could face, don't you think?" Shimada said.

Reisman just looked down and shook his head. "Not by a longshot, Alexis."

COFFEE SHOP
NASHVILLE, TENNESSEE

NemoChill was working in his "office," a Well Coffeehouse in Nashville, Tennessee. Good internet connection and not easy to track a connection back to them. They were sipping a "Spicy Snowman"—basically a cinnamon latte—and poking around the so-called back doors of company IT firewalls.

NemoChill, their screen name among a group of amateur hackers, liked the thrill of finding their way into the IT tech hubs of companies. They spent an entire week in an oil company's IT nest, as they liked to call it, before being blocked by that company's hacker firewalls. Today, they were running Brutus, a software program that guesses passwords. Brutus isn't particularly smart, but it systematically runs through thousands of password combinations every second, eventually drilling its way into a company's IT system through a back door of some kind. NemoChill decided to use a graphics processor to help speed up Brutus' work.

The process of identifying system vulnerabilities is full of endless opportunities, and NemoChill was proud that they knew most of them. Someone may have left a "back door" to a system exposed unintentionally. There is no way to quantify the different ways a hacker can launch a cyber-attack. It all comes down to a hacker's capability to imagine novel ideas and methods to break through cyber defenses and, more importantly, implement an attack quickly. Hacking is a technical game requiring a methodical and mathematical mind. NemoChill's skill then came down to IT dexterity and a lot of patience. "Systemizing," is what the cyber-security experts call it. NemoChill was good at systemizing their approach.

"What's this? Cloud computing entity. Foot, New York. What a stupid sounding name for a town." They knew what they were about to undertake was wildly illegal, but the sheer thrill of once again breaking into a place everyone said could not be broken into was the juice that kept NemoChill going.

Well, lookie here. Senior management compensation for 2019. Wow, they pay well. Let's tell the world.

With one keystroke, Trask International's pay rates for every executive became public knowledge.

Whoa, wait. Is that a "kill switch?" My lucky day. Wonder what it kills . . .

At that moment, an engineer in Trask International's cloud computing hub saw every screen go blank as every server shut down.

"What the fu . . ."

NOTES FROM THE AUTHOR

A few things about the book.

The name "Trask International" is taken from a book titled *Nobody Wants My Resume*, written in the 1970s by Donald Mancha, a pen name adopted by a coworker of mine at IBM. The book presented a humorous look at life inside a big corporation. Since I wanted to write a fictional piece and primarily demonstrate the value of crisis communications planning, I borrowed the name Trask International so as not to throw any particular company under the literary bus.

Second, the angle of the story where the shooter wants to surrender to a reporter is based on true events from May 28, 1982. Pam Coulter, a reporter for WTOP in Washington, D.C., an all-news outlet, was on her way to a hairdresser appointment that day when she was summoned by her editor to cover the story. She knew someone who worked in the IBM building and called that person's office phone. Her contact answered and said he couldn't speak because of what was going on. He suggested she call back at a different number. When she dialed the second number, she was shocked to find it was Edward Mann, the shooter, who answered. He said to her, "I'm the one. I'm the guy they want." To this day Coulter does not know if she dialed a wrong number or if her contact knew the shooter was in a nearby office. Regardless, she and Mann spoke for a few minutes. Mann even offered to surrender to her. Eventually, the intel she gathered from her phone conversation helped lead the police to Mann's location and his eventual surrender. To the police, not Coulter.

I also created most of the police interaction with the press and public because in 1982, the news coverage of an event was less ubiquitous than it is today. I learned of Mann's surrender after arriving at my apartment in time to watch the 6 p.m. local news of the story on local station WRC-TV. It was less sensational in nature than mass shooting reports are today. The coverage contained zero interviews with people who had escaped the building. No interviews with anyone standing outside watching. There wasn't even an on-camera interview with a police official. Just a five to ten second video footage of people running out of the building, and the sound accompanying that video footage was that of a police siren. After anchor Jim Vance finished talking about the shooting, he moved on to other stories, sports, and the weather. At the very end of this 30-minute broadcast, Vance announced that word had just come in that the shooter had surrendered to the police.

Also, unlike today's environment, there was no 24/7 coverage of the gunman. No extensive reporting on his home life. Little of his former employment with IBM at first, and none later when news coverage of his trial took place. Essentially, this was treated as a one-day story, and the second story would come after he appeared before a judge.

The incident did not completely vanish from the news. There were a few interviews with some people who came face-to-face with Mann, including one interview with an IBM employee who tried, unsuccessfully, to wrestle a gun from Mann's grip. Mann's weapon had jammed, and this employee used this momentary opening to try to pull it from Mann's hands. Unfortunately for him, Mann was considerably bigger than this fellow. Mann broke the employee's nose by striking him with the gunstock of the shotgun he was carrying. The strike knocked the employee to the ground and Mann continued along on his shooting rampage rather than shooting this brave individual.

But when Mann did take his own life in 1986, there was scant coverage in the press. The only clipping I could find was an Associated Press story covering the suicide by two inmates being held in the Maryland correctional system.

ABOUT SOCIAL MEDIA

The din of messages can make it challenging to maintain clarity of message. Everyone is shouting, albeit over X (nee: Twitter) all at once. And there is no one who can, at some point, speak up and yell, "One voice at a time, please!" Who shouts that order when the conversation is taking place 280 characters at a time and the others shouting are separated by an internet connection? This is a conversation among people who aren't near each other.

Social media puts a ton of information on the average person to review, digest, and make sense of. It isn't always easy. Author David Baldacci wrote *The Sixth Man*, (Grand Central Publishing, 2011) a book about a man who was on a different mental plane than anyone else. He could digest a tsunami of information and generate usable analysis for U.S. intelligence agencies to use. The twist in this story is that this man was considered mentally unstable; others who tried to replicate his digest and analysis process went insane from attempting to make sense of an avalanche of data. So having the knack of managing an unending flood of sensory input isn't what it is cracked up to be.

Nowadays, we, in a sense, must be our own sixth man, processing scores of messages and somehow making sense of it all. We don't go insane, but we can become misinformed, misled, and confused.

SOME RESOURCES

There is an extensive support system in place nowadays for anyone who is a victim of a shooting or other violent attack. I offer the following as a general resource, not as an all-encompassing database.

Sandy Hook Promise (**www.sandyhookpromise.org**) - A national nonprofit organization founded and led by several family members whose loved ones were killed at Sandy Hook Elementary School on December 14, 2012.

Victims First (**www.victimsfirst.org**) - Dedicated to helping victims of mass casualty crime.

Every Town Support Fund (**www.everytownsupportfund.org**) - A first step site directing visitors to organizations such as Moms Demand Action, Students Demand Action, and the Survivor Network.

Gun Violence Archive (**www.gunviolencearchive.org**) - A clearinghouse of information on mass shootings and other violent acts. Dynamically updated as the epidemic of violence continues.

Survivors Empowered (**www.survivorsempowered.org**) - Founded after the Aurora Colorado Theater mass shooting in 2012, this is a national organization created by survivors, for survivors, empowering survivors.

Center for Disaster Philanthropy (**www.disasterphilanthropy. org**) - The only full-time resource dedicated to helping donors maximize their impact through expert resources, community-driven grantmaking, and philanthropic consulting services.

CRISIS COMMUNICATIONS PLANS

IABC (**www.iabc.com**) - The International Association of Business Communicators runs a number of webinars and seminars on crisis communications planning.

PRSA (**www.prsa.org**) - The Public Relations Society of America's main headquarters and chapters throughout the United States offers numerous resources for crisis planning.

204 | CRISIS COMMUNICATIONS

FOOTNOTES

1. Stefan Wojcik, Pew Research Center, 5 Things to Know About Bots on Twitter, April 9, 2018.
2. Joe Turow, "The Daily You. How the new advertising industry is defining your identity and your worth," Yale University Press, 2012.
3. CNN Town Hall, Marco Rubio is asked by a Marjorie Stoneman Douglas survivor if he will stop accepting donations from the NRA. CNN, February 18, 2018.
4. Noelle C. Nelson, Valuing Employees by, Society for Human Resource Management, February 1, 2006.
5. Certified Crisis Management Professional, available via the Business Community Management Institute.
6. Study: On Twitter, false news travels faster than true stories, MIT News, March 8, 2018.
7. Twitter Blog, People coming to Twitter for news, September 12, 2022.
8. Bruce A. Williamks and Michael X. Delli Carpini, *After Broadcast News: Media Regimes, Democracy, and the New Information Environment.* New York: Cambridge University Press, 2011.
9. Sanjay Kalavar and Mihir Mysore, McKinsey crisis response steps.
10. Crisis Response | Risk & Resilience | McKinsey & Company www.mckinsey.com/capabilities/risk-and-resilience/how-we-help-clients/crisis-response.
11. Chattanooga Army Recruitment office shooting, CBS News, July 16, 2015.
12. U.S. Congressional Research Services study on defining a mass shooting.

13. Consumer Health Ratings, how much does an ER visit cost? cost of an emergency room visit, February 20, 2023.
14. Dina Amro, "This moment will not define us": Collierville Kroger reopens 7 weeks after shooting, Memphis Commercial Appeal, November 10, 2021.

APPENDIX

SAMPLE CRISIS COMMUNICATIONS PLAN

There are multiple crisis planning templates that are available for free online. Hubspot.com has several, as do some of the planning resources contacts listed earlier. What follows is a very simple crisis plan, modified from sources within HubSpot, IABC, PRSA, and elsewhere that should be adaptable to any organization.

CRISIS COMMUNICATIONS PLAN TEMPLATE

CRISIS COMMUNICATIONS STEPS

1. Notify - News of a crisis can come in from any place at any time. Everyone in an organization needs to know who to contact in the event of a crisis, regardless of the severity of said crisis.
2. Activate the plan - Again, regardless of the severity, a plan should be ready to be activated. This can be as simple as holding statements and company-wide notification of a minor (or major) disruption of business.
3. Gather the facts - Things move fast in a crisis. Have a plan - a network of contacts, if you will - where you can gather/

confirm/understand facts.

4. Formulate/deliver a response - Be firm and consistent.
5. Identify stakeholders - Know these players in advance. Who is most impacted? Whose influence affects the enterprise?
6. Deliver messages - Establish clear and consistent channels - press, social media, web, and more.
7. Monitor and correct - Not every message will be clear. Be prepared to clarify, restate, and repeat messages.
8. Update and follow up - Keep everyone in the loop. There is no such thing as over communicating.
9. Debrief and evaluate - Every crisis is different. Every response is different. Look at your response. Be objective and identify what did and did not work.
10. Recovery - What steps are taken to bring business back to normal (or a new normal)?

ESCALATION FRAMEWORK
WHERE YOU CAN DETERMINE THE SEVERITY OF A CRISIS.

Level 1
This is the highest level of crisis escalation and should involve an all-hands-on-deck approach. Describe this situation as immediate to your customers, partners, employees, and/or all stakeholders.

Examples:
Typically, they involve violence, executive misconduct, or a long-term threat of damage to your customers, the company and/or stakeholders.

- Person/Team #1: Task or action
- Person/Team #2: Task or action
- Person/Team #3: Task or action

Level 2

Level 2 presents a moderate potential risk or impact on business operations, customer success, and/or company reputation.

Examples:
These may include the risk of immediate major customer churn.

- Person/Team #1: Task or action
- Person/Team #2: Task or action
- Person/Team #3: Task or action

Level 3

This is unlikely to pose a long-term risk to or impact business operations, customer success, and/or company reputation, but the team should still be on the same page for responding.

Examples:
Instances can include an executive leave of absence, a moderate customer impact that can easily be (or already has been) remedied, or rumors (such as a merger/acquisition).

- Person/Team #1: Task or action
- Person/Team #2: Task or action
- Person/Team #3: Task or action

Level 4

This is where most crises will fall into. They tend to be slightly bigger versions of day-to-day issues that may need a bit of extra effort to be fully resolved or addressed.

Examples:
Some examples include a short outage with no impact on support or an angry customer on Twitter.

- Person/Team #1: Task or action
- Person/Team #2: Task or action
- Person/Team #3: Task or action

INCIDENT RESPONSE TEAM

Describe the purpose of this team, why it was assembled, and what it is responsible for doing.

MAINTAIN A FIRST LINE OF DEFENSE

Identify the key players to be informed once the company is aware of the crisis. The list should include the names of the individuals, the team/department those people are members of, and how to best communicate to each member individually. If there is an internal chat system or group email for the whole team, list that here as well.

- Person/Team #1: Email and/or Phone Number
- Person/Team #2: Email and/or Phone Number
- Person/Team #3: Email and/or Phone Number
- Person/Team #4: Email and/or Phone Number
- Group Email/Communication Method: List Here

GREATER RESPONSE TEAM

Identify with names and 24-hour contact information who is responsible for what. Parties that make up a greater incident response team may include the following:

- Communications

- Customer Support
- Legal
- Partner Communications
- Social Media
- Customer Marketing
- People Ops and H.R.
- Product/Engineering
- Executives
- Security

CRISIS TEAM - ROLES AND RESPONSIBILITIES

The roles and responsibilities will be different for each business or organization. Identify the team and explain their roles (making sure there is universal agreement on those roles).
Typical team members include:

- **Communications**
- **Customer Support**
- **Legal**
- **Social Media/Marketing (may be a part of communications)**
- **Human resources**
- **Product**
- **Other**

NOTE: Maintain 24/7 contact information (business phone, personal phone, email) for everyone on the team.

CRISIS MANAGEMENT PROCESS

Phase 1: ALERT
Outline the actions necessary to ensure the response team is

notified and put to work as soon as possible. Emphasize that if someone is unsure if he or she should alert the team that he or she should, just in case.

Your alert system can be as simple as an internal chat system channel or email alias.

Phase 2: ASSESS
Once the Response Team has been notified, what happens next? Explain how the team will assess the (potential) crisis, gather any available information, classify the incident via the escalation framework above, and prepare to take subsequent action.
Here are some questions to answer to get you started:

- What happened?
- Where and when?
- Who was affected?
- Who is involved?
- When did we learn about the incident?
- What is the impact/likely impact?
- Is there any immediate danger?
- Do we understand the entire issue?

Phase 3: ACTIVATE
Describe how the response team will communicate with the appropriate team members for their tasks and/or with external stakeholders for specific messaging.

In the box below, write out a few common tasks expected in a crisis situation, and delegate that task to a responsible party in the form of a department or an individual. These tasks could include incident response team communication, initial external messaging, gathering/monitoring information, finding a meeting space, team check-in cadence, etc.

ACTION WHO IS RESPONSIBLE?

Example Action   Responsible Party
Example Action   Responsible Party
Example Action   Responsible Party
Example Action   Responsible Party
Example Action   Responsible Party

Phase 4: ADMINISTER

Determine how the Response Team will continue to assess, address, and resolve the incident. This includes communication to stakeholders, employees, and customers if appropriate, as well as developing a timeline, seeking external legal or technical assistance, moderating and responding to media, and updating your crisis communication plan. This section should address the steps for any crisis, whether long-term or short-term.

Example Action   Responsible Party
Example Action   Responsible Party
Example Action   Responsible Party
Example Action   Responsible Party
Example Action   Responsible Party

Part 5: REVIEW

Once the immediacy of the crisis has dissipated, regroup as a team to go over your process for crisis management, response, and communication. Consider what changes should be made and update this plan with those changes.

If there are any outstanding issues that need to be addressed, or if further monitoring of communication/media is necessary, delegate individuals or departments to manage those tasks.
Maintaining an Effective Response Plan

Keep the plan fresh to make sure your response is timely and effective. Schedule times to review the plan and make adjustments to the plan as necessary.

TRASK INTERNATIONAL, BETHESDA BUILDING FLOOR PLAN

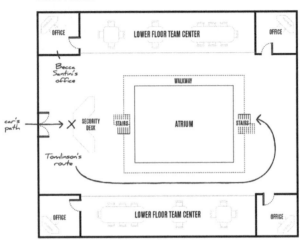

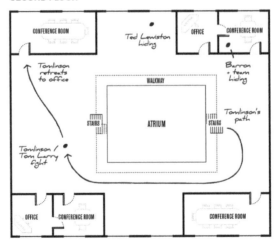

TRASK CRISIS COMMUNICATIONS TEAM

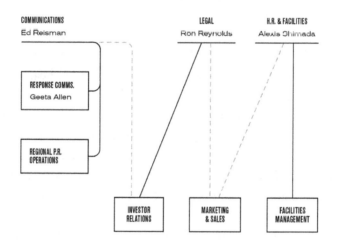

ACKNOWLEDGEMENTS

Just as no crisis plan is ever created on its own, no book is a sole endeavor. I have the privilege of working with the terrific folks at Beaufort Books – Megan Trank, Emma St. John, Alexa Schmidt, Kaylee Lovato, and Caitlin Daly. It was Caitlin who undertook the herculean task of copy editing my work. For any headaches I caused you, Caitlin, I apologize and thank you.

A special thank you to Amy Saal of Untuck, a wonderful design firm, for creating the graphics in this book, and to Frances Fragela Rivera for the cover design. Early on, Beaufort asked me for my thoughts on a cover design and, honest-to-goodness, my initial thought was (and still is), "I'm a word guy. I'll let the designers do their work."

And a thank you to the scores of communications professionals I have encountered in my 40-plus years in P.R. and who I interviewed for the book. Your intelligence and insights into crisis planning are a big part of what goes into this book.